Hillary and Vince

A story of love, death, and cover-up

Dean W. Arnold

www.DeanArnold.org

For further information, contact author at dean@deanarnold.org

About the Author

U.S. Senator Bob Corker (now chairman of the Senate Foreign Relations Committee) says, "Dean Arnold has a unique way of capturing the essence of an issue and communicating it through his clear but compelling style of writing."

That endorsement highlighted Arnold's book *America's Trail of Tears*, 1st Runner-up of the Eric Hoffer Legacy Award.

Newsweek Editor and Pulitzer prize-winning author Jon Meacham said Arnold's book *Old Money, New South* was "well worth reading." The book traces the billionaire families of Coca-Cola bottling and their 100-year reign over the city where Coke bottling started, Chattanooga, Tennessee.

Arnold's movie script "The Wizard and the Lion" on the dynamic relationship between authors J.R.R. Tolkien (*The Lord of the Rings*) and C.S. Lewis (*The Chronicles of Narnia*) was endorsed by the Oxford C.S. Lewis Society.

His full feature documentary *Harriet's Secret: a progressive marriage in the 1890s* premiered at the Chattanooga IMAX Theater October, 2014.

First a writer, Arnold is part documentarian, part theologian and philosopher, and part artist—and hopes not to be just a part Christian. "I keep vacillating between creative projects and expose's," he said. "I've found my voice as a writer, but my subject matter is still a moving target."

Vince Foster with Hillary and Bill Clinton

To Robert Kwasnik and Brian Kelly

1.

Patrick Knowlton had no intention of being a key witness in one of recent history's most celebrated crime scenes when he drove to a park off the road to relieve himself in July of 1993.

He had just finished a construction job and was driving past Fort Marcy Park near Washington D.C. on his way to a cabin he owned where he planned to do more carpentry work.

Like many skilled laborers, Patrick was a registered Democrat.[1] He moonlighted as a private investigator and a security guard, and on a few occasions was called to work at the White House. Once, he got his picture taken with President Clinton.

Otherwise, he avoided politics and other controversial matters. He grinded along with an Eastern lunch bucket work ethic, forged in Syracuse where his single mom raised him and several siblings with the help of welfare. Work was now a privilege.[2]

Patrick was stunned when the Evening News reported that White House counsel Vince Foster, the President and First lady's close friend, had been found dead earlier in Fort Marcy Park. The early reports were suicide, but Patrick had seen a suspicious character in the parking lot that afternoon.

Patrick has always been keenly observant, and he saw 4:30 pm on his clock when he drove into Fort Marcy's lot and pulled up next to an old brown Honda with Arkansas tags on his left. Two spaces to his right, a man in a blue car, facing toward the driveway, rolled down his window and stared menacingly. "It was a 'get the hell out of here' kind of look,"[3] said Patrick. He would have likely done just that, except his bladder demanded attention.

He hopped out of the car and the sinister man—well dressed, Hispanic or Middle Eastern, early thirties—also got out of his car. Fearing he may be mugged, Patrick stopped at an historical marker, and pretended to read it. The man leaned on his car roof and kept staring, so Patrick headed for the nearest tree. When he returned, he walked around the brown Honda, noticing details such as a leather briefcase and a suit jacket folded over the driver's seat. "Maybe I'm keeping the guy from breaking into that car," Patrick thought, as the man kept staring. He was grateful to drive away unharmed.[4]

Patrick Knowlton

He may not even have mentioned it to Kathryn, his girlfriend, had the Evening News not given the incident new meaning. "I saw the guy's car," said Patrick. "I can't believe a big time lawyer was driving that old heap." They discussed it for a while, and she persuaded him that it was his duty to report what he had seen to the police.[5] He called after midnight, but the officer he spoke with was rude and uninterested. He could have left it there, but Patrick decided to call again the next morning and was able to tell his story to Detective John Rolla. He thanked Patrick, but never called him back. The news continued to proclaim Foster's death a suicide, and Patrick was happy to leave it at that.

The FBI called nine months later for an interview. He told them about the suspicious man in the Park and said he could easily identify him. But they were interested in the Honda. They showed him a picture of a late 80s gray Honda. Was that it? No, it was early 80s and rust brown, Patrick said. They showed him several more pictures. Still no success.

The FBI agent, Larry Monroe, threw the pictures down on his desk in disgust and called in his partner, William Colombel. "The Park Police sent us the wrong photos! Knowlton says it's brown."[6]

Pat was called in for a second interview. He was happy to oblige, but was having a tough day. The evening before, someone had taken a crowbar in downtown D.C. and smashed the headlights and tail lights out of his restored Peugeot 504.[7] But the FBI men were friendly. They assured him they didn't want to taint his testimony.

"Are you sure the Honda was brown?"

"Yes."

"Could the sun through the trees have affected your view?"

"No."

"What if we told you that the other witnesses saw a newer model gray Honda?"

"No. I saw what I saw."

After asking him the same questions again and again, they told him not to talk about what he had seen. "The Foster family is very upset about all this," said Agent Monroe. "I'm sure you understand."[8] Patrick refused an opportunity later to share his story on Gordon Liddy's radio show.[9] He was confused by the FBI's strange behavior, but was confident they would get to the bottom of it.

2.

The death of Vince Foster had caught the attention of reporter Ambrose Evans-Pritchard, head of the Washington bureau for the prestigious *London Telegraph* newspaper. Many questions had emerged on Foster. Why wouldn't the Park Police release their report? Why was the death immediately ruled a suicide? Why did top Clinton aides block police from searching Foster's office, and why was a file called "Whitewater" removed from his office? Such questions had forced Attorney General Janet Reno to appoint a Special Prosecutor, New York attorney Robert Fiske, to re-examine the suspicious death.

In a 60-page preliminary report, Fiske ruled the death a suicide. Patrick's name did not appear in the Fiske report. He was only identified as a witness who saw Foster's Honda and a suit jacket "folded over the passenger seat."[10] The *London Telegraph* reporter decided to examine this witness's full FBI statement (called "FBI 302s"), which had been made available by the Senate Banking Committee which had held a cursory one-day hearing on the Foster death and accepted Fiske's verdict of suicide.

The two agents who interviewed Patrick, Larry Monroe and William Colombel, also testified before the Senate committee. When Ambrose examined their 302 Report of Patrick, he was surprised to read about a menacing dark man at the scene. Ambrose hired a private detective to track down Patrick.[11]

Patrick was unaware of the Fiske investigation. He told Ambrose he had never seen his 302 and was eager to read it. But enthusiasm turned to anger when the FBI report said Patrick could not "further identify" the sinister man and "would be unable to recognize him in the future."

"The bastards! That's an outright lie. I told them I could pick him out of a line-up."

The FBI 302 also described the car Patrick had clearly observed as "a 1988 to 1990 brown or rust brown Honda with Arkansas plates."

"I never said that. I want it on the record I never said that," Patrick shouted as Ambrose listened. "I told them it was an older model, '83 or '84. I was certain about it. I told them I couldn't believe a White House lawyer would be driving a beaten-up old thing like that."

The Fiske Report concluded that Patrick Knowlton "saw nothing unusual or suspicious in the park that day."

Ambrose planned to run an international story on these stunning revelations. A steaming Patrick Knowlton was willing to be quoted. He normally ducked from controversy, and he realized a couple of FBI agents might get upset. But he wanted the record set straight. He provided a detailed description of the dark, menacing man to an artist hired by the *Telegraph*. It was printed on the front page with the title: "Death in the Park: Is this the Killer?" [12]

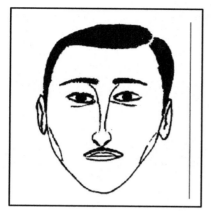

Forensic drawing of man at park.

3.

Hillary's pet name for him was "Vincenco Fosterini."[13] He was the secretive, behind-the-scenes type. Their getaways during work hours at the Rose Law Firm included lunch while watching lingerie shows.[14] She even hired a belly dancer[15] for him on his birthday.

Hillary Clinton regularly confided in Vince Foster while her husband conducted affair after affair during their troubled marriage in Arkansas. Vince was commonly known to be Hillary's closest friend, but many others knew them to be lovers.

"It was an accepted fact that Hillary and Vince were sleeping with other," said Dr. Michael Galster, whose wife Vali was a close friend of Hillary's. The couple mixed in the Clinton's social circles. "Hillary and Vince's love affair was an open secret," he said.[16]

While the national media trumpeted the revelations of former Clinton bodyguards about the Governor's many sexual liaisons, little was heard about their talk of Hillary's affair. State Troopers Larry Patterson and Roger Perry related how Vince would show up at the Governor's mansion in the evening like clockwork[17] whenever Bill Clinton traveled. They also escorted Hillary and Vince to a remote cabin out in the woods.[18]

"Everybody knew about Hillary and Vince,"[19] said Jim McDougal, the man who persuaded the Clintons to buy property called Whitewater.

Trooper L. D. Brown was Bill Clinton's closest bodyguard, since he was an intelligent man. (He later studied for a doctorate in political science.). "Hillary and Vince were deeply in love," said Brown.[20] "I saw them locked in each other's arms, deep kissing, nuzzling." He was more blunt when describing an incident to the *American Spectator*. Hillary and Vince were on a walk and "running tongues down each other's throats."[21]

L. D. Brown says Hillary gave him this advice: "There are some things you have to get outside your marriage that you can't get in it." The trooper has no doubt about Vince and Hillary's affair. "I was there. I saw it."[22]

Bill Clinton with L. D. Brown

She had not always wanted or needed to look outside her marriage. When Hillary first met Bill Clinton at Yale Law School, she fell in love quickly. It started when Hillary noticed Bill looking at her constantly in a study room. Finally, she crossed the room and held out her hand. "Look, if you're going to keep staring at me and I'm going to keep staring back, we might as well introduce ourselves."[23]

Bill was surprised. But he liked her spunk and intellect. He was emotional and sensitive, providing everything she had craved but failed to receive from her father, Hugh Rodham.

A former drill sergeant, Rodham was "as rough as a corn cob, gruff as he could be,"[24] said a family friend. "Head up, chin in, chest out, stomach in!"[25] he would order his daughter if he noticed bad posture. Biographer Carl Bernstein calls him a "sour, unfulfilled man," a difficult character. Others simply describe him as abusive. "Don't let the doorknob hit your ass on the way out,"[26] he was known to quip to his wife if she ever showed some nerve.

When Hillary brought home straight A's, he told her the school must be easy. When his son quarterbacked the team to victory, competing 10 of 11 passes, he said he ought to have gone 11 for 11.[27]

By the time she was in law school, Hillary was many years into her drive to impress the world with major achievement. But Bill Clinton provided instantaneous affirmation. The gushing leader famous for feeling the world's pain was focusing his master emotional skills on Hillary during their early years. Soon they were engaged.

Bill, however, had the ability to connect with more than one woman at a time. He had never wavered from his early ambition to run for office in Arkansas. His ambition was to become President some day,[28] and Hillary embraced his goal. She also desired the office for herself.[29]

"From an early age, she dreamed of living in the White House," said Hillary's high school youth minister.[30] College friends talked about Hillary being the first female president, and McGovern campaign colleague Betsy Wright felt the same way. "I was less interested in Bill's political future than in Hillary's," she said. "I was obsessed with how far Hillary might go, with her mixture of brilliance, ambition, and self-assuredness."[31]

When Hillary heard that Bill had a girlfriend in Little Rock, she was devastated. Despite her ambitions in Washington D.C. where she was assisting prosecutors in the Watergate Hearings, she packed up and moved to Arkansas.

"If she comes to Arkansas," Bill told friends before she arrived, "it's going to be my state, my future. She could be president someday. She could go to any state and be elected to the Senate. If she comes to Arkansas, she'll be on my turf."[32]

When she arrived, Hillary heard more about the other woman Bill was seeing, known among the campaign staff as "the college girl." In fact, she thought *she* was his fiancé.[33] Hillary asked her brother Hughie to move to

Little Rock, and he was dispatched to chase off the college girl.

"That's exactly what he did," said Paul Fray, a campaign aid. "She came to me and said, 'I want you to stop this son of bitch bothering me.'"[34] The girl eventually left. Bill and Hillary married.

4.

Patrick Knowlton had not been contacted by the current grand jury investigating the Vince Foster death. After the FBI interviews, no one had ever contacted him. Ambrose pointed this out in his international article. The day the article hit in the United States, the grand jury issued a subpoena to Patrick Knowlton to appear for its investigation. Patrick was happy to oblige. FBI Agent Russell Bransford delivered the subpoena to Patrick's apartment and left his card.[35]

But a couple of days later a strange thing happened. Patrick and Kathryn were taking their normal walk in downtown D.C. when a man in a suit walked by, stared at Patrick with a menacing look, and then talked into his sleeve. Some kind of officer. Whatever.

A few seconds later another man walked by and did the same thing. They were staring specifically at Patrick, but Kathryn, a Ph D. not known to over-react, was also alarmed.

As they walked further, a man—this time casually dressed—turned toward them and stared for 15 seconds as they walked by. Patrick took his girlfriend's arm and crossed the street. He saw more men. "This can't be happening," he thought. But it was. He decided they needed to walk swiftly home. Even more men, mostly in suits, stared them down—some even brushed up next to them--and a car also followed them slowly. Later, they recounted 25 different men who harassed them.[36]

They called FBI Agent Bransford but heard nothing back. They called the grand jury investigation, but the receptionist laughed under her breath. In fairness, it was a bizarre story. A reporter with the *New York Post*, Christopher Ruddy, came to Patrick's apartment and saw the men outside. They took several photos of them. After taking Patrick outside for a brief moment to confirm he and Kathryn's story, Ruddy called Ambrose.

"You're not going to believe what's going on here. There's a surveillance net of at least thirty people harassing Patrick. I've never seen anything like it in my life," he said.

When Ruddy left, a loud knock sounded from the door. Patrick opened it, but no one was there. This happened several times. The phone also rang, but they kept hanging up. He called Ambrose.

"I can't take it anymore. I want out of this."

"Stay calm, don't let these criminals get to you. You can stay at my place."

When Ambrose arrived, the men had left and Patrick and Kathryn were calmer. He decided to stay put.

Ambrose Evans-Pritchard

Two days later, Agent Bransford finally stopped by to talk to Patrick. Someone at FBI had called earlier and hinted that the problem was concocted by his reporter friends to sell newspapers.[37] Patrick was getting fed up, and asked Bransford to call beforehand so he could have an attorney present when they talked.

"You don't need an attorney," he said.

"Well, I think I do."

Bransford failed to provide the courtesy call, and the two sat in the living room as Patrick took a long time to recount the whole story. Meanwhile, Bransford was nodding, half smiling, even smirking and mocking.

Patrick stopped and looked at him, confused and bewildered.

The agent broke the silence. "You know, Agent Monroe and Agent Colombel are good friends of mine."

Patrick realized he was being "protected" by a friend of the two agents exposed in the *London Telegraph* article.

Patrick got to the point. "Can I trust you, Mr. Bransford?"

The FBI agent leaned forward. "That's a good question. I don't know."

Patrick told him to get the hell out of his house.[38]

5.

Bachelors do their own laundry.

In the past few years, Patrick had run into John Clarke in the laundry room, a good-looking young guy, an attorney. At one point, Patrick needed some help on a car insurance issue.

"Can't help you. I'm a criminal attorney," John said.[39]

But when things heated up with the FBI, Patrick contacted John, who took a serious interest in his predicament. Over time, Patrick and John were befriended by a noted Beltway figure, Reed Irvine, founder of Accuracy in Media. Irvine was a grandfatherly type who had taken special interest in the Foster mystery. He even appeared on *Nightline* to discuss it with Ted Koppel.

Reed was examining Fort Marcy Park one day when Hugh Turley stopped in by happenstance. The two met, and Irvine's charisma convinced Hugh to help him. Hugh had a flexible schedule—he was a children's entertainer who made kids laugh and amused adults as "Turley the Magician." Those magic skills made him a crack researcher as well, with a keen ability to notice what was being hidden in reports. He befriended Patrick and John, and the three became a trio with a mission, under the guiding hand of Reed Irvine.[40]

Patrick's new friends assured him that he would be safe and that justice would prevail. Patrick and Kathryn settled down over time.

Patrick found out he wasn't the only one whose testimony had been altered. And his team discovered that Patrick's bizarre encounter on the streets was actually a known FBI tactic.[41] It had been used a number of times during the days of Martin Luther King's civil rights uprisings and the days of McCarthy's communist probes. Retired intelligence officers explained the purpose: to discredit a witness as a nut before he appears before a grand jury and to destabilize him so his testimony is uncertain.[42]

John Clarke

But why would so many FBI agents care so much about his testimony? As the trio of Patrick the witness, John the attorney, and Hugh the researcher rolled up their sleeves to examine the evidence, the precise answer was not immediately forthcoming. But many other strange questions and oddities emerged.

Hugh Turley

While the Senate had only held one day of hearings, they had also collected thousands of documents and examined many of the key players under oath. The trio learned that Patrick wasn't the only one who'd seen a brown car. A couple enjoying a tryst in the woods had observed the same brown Honda. According to their FBI reports collected by the Senate, this couple also saw a large, bare-chested, unkempt man with long, blonde hair and beard looking at the Honda's engine. The blonde man later walked into the woods where Foster's body was found. But Fiske's report leaves all this out, and only mentions that "neither heard a gunshot while in the park or observed anything unusual."[43]

The old brown Honda seen by Patrick and the couple didn't fit the description of the official car, a gray car. And if Vince Foster didn't drive his car to the park, the official story makes no sense.

The photo taken by the Park Police showed a 1989 gray Honda. It's a close-up; you can't tell the car's location. Oddly, the license plate was whited out and the windscreen did not show a White House pass.[44]

A woman whose Mercedes had broken down and was looking for a phone was quoted by the Fiske Report as seeing a "light gray" car. But she told Ambrose it was "tannish brown." The medical examiner told Ambrose he saw a "beat up orange compact."[45]

One Senator did have a simple question about the car. But he really didn't get an answer.

SENATOR D'AMATO: . . . Did the FBI ever attempt to determine what time Mr. Foster departed the White House and do we know if the Secret Service keeps a vehicle exit log?

MR. MONROE: Sir, all of our information right now suggested that Mr. Foster departed the White House on July 20th at approximately 1:00 p.m. Whether or not that departure time was based on interviews or a log by the Secret Service, I am not aware of that, sir, but we know that he left about that time.

FBI Agents Larry Monroe and William Colombel

SENATOR D'AMATO: Would you be able—I mean, this investigation, as it relates to the circumstances surrounding Mr. Foster's death, wouldn't you look at the vehicle departure log to determine what time he may have left? Isn't that a routine thing?

MR. COLOMBEL: Senator, I don't believe the vehicle was logged out of the White House. I don't believe it was parked in an area where it would have been logged out of the White House. We confirmed that he left around 1:00 to 1:15 p.m.[46]

The White House, of course, has the world's finest system for tracking the people and vehicles that come and go. But the FBI hadn't bothered to explore why Foster's car wasn't on the logs that day. Neither had they bothered to track down other evidence like the long blonde hairs found on Foster's undershirt, pants, belt, socks and shoes.[47]

SENATOR BENNETT: I'm just interested to know what you learned about the blonde hairs.

MR. MONROE: The source of this hair could have been boundless. It could have been from his residence. It could have been from his automobile, which was used quite often by his children.[48]

So the FBI didn't bother to try and match the hairs with a family member or colleague. Neither did they bother to find the one fingerprint found on the gun. It wasn't Foster's.[49] But the print was never run through the FBI database.[50] Neither did they check for fingerprints on Foster's clothing or car.

Patrick and his friends learned some other strange facts about the gun found at the death scene. The Fiske Report identified it as a .38 caliber black revolver.[51] It had two serial numbers because it was two different pieces—a barrel and a butt—making it more difficult to track. And because it was made in 1913, it was untraceable.[52]

But one of the first medics on the scene didn't see a revolver, the kind of gun where you spin the bullets like in Russian Roulette. Paramedic Richard Arthur, an ex-army man, was "100 percent sure"[53] it wasn't a revolver. Perhaps a nine millimeter pistol,[54] he said. Square, not round like a revolver. He drew a picture of both kinds of guns[55] to prove his point.

However, the Fiske Report uses Foster's wife and sister as its primary evidence for identifying the gun. "(Sister) Sharon Bowman identified it as appearing very similar to the one their father kept in his bedside table, specifically recalling the pattern of the grip," Fiske writes.[56]

Fiske artfully calls the gun similar, but does not say it's the actual gun. Because it wasn't. She had only seen a picture of it. "Sharon thought she would be able to recognize it, but she really couldn't," her husband, Lee Bowman, told reporter Ambrose.[57]

Fiske left out the statements of Sharon's son, Lee Foster Bowman, the family gun expert who would go hunting with his grandfather. His FBI 302 stated that the gun at the death scene was an "old piece of junk" and looked nothing like his grandfather's silver-antique. "He didn't remember the black handle and the dark color of the metal," the report confirms.[58]

Neither did Lisa Foster recognize the black gun she was shown. She remembered an old silver gun, not a black one, which had been packed away in their home back in Little Rock. "Not the gun she thought it must be. Silver six-gun, large barrel,"[59] wrote the Park Police captain a few days after Vince died.

FBI photo of gun allegedly with Foster

Then how could Fiske write that "the gun looked similar to the one she had seen in their home in Arkansas and that she had brought to Washington"?[60] Once again, a doctored FBI 302 helped, and Fiske conveniently leaves out colors. Conducted a year later, this FBI interview states that "Lisa Foster believes the gun found at Fort Marcy Park may be the silver gun which she brought with her other belongings when she permanently moved to Washington."[61] The FBI agents failed to remind her that the official gun was black. This second time around, they showed her "a silver colored handgun," according to a 1994 Senate Report.[62]

6.

Bill's mom complained about Hillary's lack of makeup and strange appearance. Hillary was insecure physically and did not try to compete with the Southern belles that attracted her husband. Bill's attraction to her was intellectual, as well as a shared ambition. For many years, she wore pants or plain dresses, large coke-bottle eyeglasses and frizzy hair.[63]

Over time, the politically minded couple settled into an arrangement where Bill's infidelities were ignored or overlooked. Early on, Hillary had joined the Rose Law Firm in Arkansas. Top litigator Vincent Foster took the fascinating Ivy League hippy under his wing.

Back at the Governor's mansion, troopers once overheard a yelling match after Bill returned from yet another tryst. "I need to be fucked more than twice a year!" they heard Hillary scream.[64]

Eventually, Hillary and Vince were seeing each other regularly, sometimes enjoying lingerie shows over lunch. After years of putting up with an unfaithful man, Hillary had resolved to stay married, refocusing on the national potential of the relationship, something she and Bill had discussed for years: the Presidency. On July 15, 1987, Governor Bill Clinton was scheduled to announce his bid for President.

But crisis hit when this remaining benefit of Hillary's marriage failed her. Sexual indiscretions, from Roosevelt to JFK had always been off limits to the press. But in May of 1997, leading Democrat candidate Gary Hart dropped out of the race after revelations of his affair with beautiful Donna Rice, age 27. Clips of the two flirting with each other before boarding a yacht called "Monkey Business" fed the media frenzy. The old rules were gone, and candidates' sex lives were now fair game.

Bill's affairs were now poised to ruin Hillary's entire life. His romps, past and current, included former Miss America Elizabeth Ward Gracen, local belle Dolly Kyle Browning, former Miss Arkansas Sally Perdue, and cabaret singer Gennifer Flowers, among several others. Hillary dispatched loyal chief of staff Betsy Wright to drum up a list of them all. Betsy presented a list of 15 women to Bill,[65] along with the locations of their dalliances.

"Now, I want you to tell me the truth about every one," she said. When it was over, she advised him not to run. The politically astute Clinton knew she was right.

In a few days, Bill Clinton was scheduled to formally announce his campaign at the Exelsior Hotel in Little Rock. Hollywood celebrities, national media outlets, and close friends were flying in from across the country to witness the historic moment. Instead, they heard the Governor announce his withdrawal for family reasons. Chelsea was too young. A national photo caught Hillary wiping a tear from her eye.[66]

Most biographies admit that Hillary Clinton seriously considered divorce during their days in Little Rock. But at this crucial point in the marriage agreement, Hillary changed her outlook. She would never again allow Bill's women to block their ambitions. She would not confront him and force him to stop. Rather, she would monitor his activities and keep the girls at bay. The media would never have a chance to know.

Vince Foster kept the list for Hillary,[67] and eventually helped her hire private detectives, both to monitor the activities and warn the women if they talked.

Vince Foster at the Rose Law Firm

7.

By now, Patrick, John, and Hugh were spending hours and hours together each day on the mystery of Vince Foster's death. They examined documents late into the night, sometimes at John's law office, sometimes at Patrick's apartment, but more often at John's efficiency in downtown D.C. All kinds of papers would be taped up on the walls while the trinity of detectives searched for clues. Discussion continued over dinner or over a late-night breakfast.

Patrick did not care for his experience as a targeted witness and could easily have walked away. But he also abhorred the idea that injustices were apparently being committed against witnesses in this Foster case. Also, the more they researched, the more they found blatant cover-ups and falsifications. Patrick found it appalling. They all did.

John was convinced Patrick's harassment would make a powerful legal case. He urged him to file suit. On the other hand, Patrick realized that such an action would make him an official combatant of the FBI and executive branch of the U.S. Government. He already knew what it felt like to be a marked man.

John explained that the lawsuit could also challenge the official story of Foster's death. Through the judicial system, Patrick could systematically and scientifically examine the primary evidence and witnesses at the scene.

This lawsuit just might crack the case. But a lot was at stake for Patrick, personally, if he chose to go that route.[68]

They decided to gather more evidence first. While the 302 forms behind the Fiske Report were very revealing, they needed more. All FBI interviews start with the handwritten notes of the agents, from which the 302 is written. These notes are public information and Patrick and friends were certain the notes would be powerful.

But just because they are public information does not mean they are available. Attempts to obtain them were blocked. In order to get them, a Freedom of Information Act lawsuit (FOIA) would have to be filed. The Executive Branch had a way of keeping secrets.

Even without the notes, the evidence regarding the entrance and exit wound on Foster's head was shocking. The official report says Foster shot himself in the mouth and left a gaping 1.25 inch hole in the backside of his head. "There is no other trauma identified that would suggest a circumstance other than a suicide," concluded the Fiske Report. "It is exceedingly unlikely that an individual of Mr. Foster's physical stature could have been overcome by an assailant inflicting an interoral gunshot wound without a struggle and there not to have been some other injury sustained at the time."[69]

Fort Marcy Park

Problem is, of the 26 people at the death scene, no one noticed a mouth wound or an exit wound in the skull.[70] But several saw a neck wound, just what you might expect if an assassin was pressing a gun up against a taller man like Foster.[71]

The medical examiner on the scene, Donald Haut, mentions no wound on the back of the head, but did see "trauma to the neck" [72] caused by a "low velocity weapon."[73] Paramedic Arthur was more clear. "I saw a small—what appeared to be a small gunshot wound here near the jawline," he told the Senate Banking Committee in sworn deposition.[74]

Why would such testimony remain unreported? Arthur goes on to explain why. "Lt. Bianchi told me from orders higher up that I'm not allowed to talk to anybody about this if I value my job."[75]

If Foster was in fact shot with a lower caliber weapon in the neck, where did the bullet go? Detective John Rolla testified that he gloved up and probed the back of Foster's head. He felt a "mushy spot,"[76] but no exit wound. By the time the Senate Committee deposed him, he seemed surprised about the Fiske Report's claim of a large, 1.25 inch exit hole.

"I still can't believe that the hole -- it's a small hole. They may put their finger through it, that's a big hole. His head was not blown out... I probed his head and there was no big hole there. There was no big blowout. There weren't brains running all over the place. There was blood in there. There was a mushy spot. I initially thought the bullet might still be in his head."[77]

Rolla's instincts may have been correct.

8.

Patrick wanted to get the handwritten notes behind Detective Rolla's FBI 302 statement where he talked about the back of the head. But even without this material, the mound of evidence was growing. Patrick continued to talk with John and Hugh about filing a lawsuit. It would include charges of harassment as well as spell out the contradictions in the primary evidence such as the gun, the car, and the neck wound.

After the great shock of being targeted and harassed by the FBI that day, Patrick now felt more hopeful that justice might be done. In fact, he was becoming more comfortable with the role of helping lead efforts to expose a great cover-up in the system. The United States Government had been a godsend to Patrick and his family when they grew up surviving on welfare. He knew it to be good at its core.

So one beautiful Spring day, he and his friends walked up to the courthouse in Washington D.C. and handed the clerk a lawsuit.[78] As they continued their search for evidence, a big bonus developed. A Freedom of Information Act lawsuit had shaken loose the FBI's handwritten notes.[79]

Many questions were answered. The lady in the Mercedes, according to her FBI 302, had seen a "light gray" Honda. But team Knowlton learned the truth: the handwritten notes make no mention of it. Park Police

Officer Franz Ferstl's 302 mentions a "late model, light colored" car. But those handwritten notes mention nothing as well. The notes of Haut's interview mention an orange car, but the 302 does not.[80]

An exit wound appears in the Fiske Report thanks to the doctor at the Fairfax County morgue, Julian Orenstein, whose 302 says his "purpose for lifting the body by the shoulders was to locate and observe the exit wound on the decedent's head." Cleverly written, it doesn't actually say he observed an exit wound.[81] The handwritten notes say nothing about an exit wound and nothing about lifting the body to find one.[82] It had been added wholecloth. A call from Ambrose about the exit wound to Dr. Orenstein confirmed it. He was surprised the Fiske Report implied an exit wound. "I never saw one directly," he said.[83]

But while Fiske had no trouble proclaiming a large exit wound that no one saw, he just as easily dismissed a wound that several saw. Regarding Dr. Haut's report of "trauma to the neck" apparently caused by a bullet, Fiske writes: "The photographs taken at the crime scene conclusively show there were no such wounds."[84]

Photographs. Patrick and friends learned a great deal about photos made and not made and photos kept and lost. They also learned that something bigger than the FBI may be behind the cover-up. Patrick was interested to know what the handwritten notes would say about Detective Rolla's examination of the back of Foster's head. It reads "Back of head . . ." and then the rest of the paragraph is marked out by black magic marker. Redacted. Why?[85]

Detective John Rolla

The Executive Branch is allowed to keep things secret, to withhold or redact documents, in order to protect someone's privacy or to protect national security. How is the back of Vince Foster's head an issue of national security? Or is a crime being hidden in the name of executive privilege?

The license plate of Foster's alleged gray car was also redacted.[86] As was Lisa Foster's 302 when she told the FBI about Vince driving his two grown children to work before he headed to the White House on the day of his death.[87] National security or cover-up? And who is giving the FBI the authority to redact?

9.

Even with all these questions, with all the unexamined evidence and negligence of the investigating authorities, official Washington was more than ready to get the issue behind them. Senator Christopher Dodd (D-CT) called the accusations of foul play "obscene."[88] Those doubting the official story were regularly called "Foster crazies."

Reed Irvine appeared on *Nightline*, but Ted Koppel made it clear that doubting the official story made you a conspiracy nut. "Let's assume for the sake of argument that it were true," he said to Reed (whom he acknowledged as sometimes exasperating but "always honest"). "One would have to conclude that everyone who investigated this case, and all those who subsequently read all the reports, would have to be in collusion. I'm wondering what reason you might think would bring Democrats and Republicans, critics and friends of the Clinton administration, to conspire to come to that conclusion."[89]

Had Reed been given time enough to respond, he could have provided one clear example: the coroner. He alone is the only person on record to have seen a large exit hole in the back of Foster's head. Fiske bases his opinion on Coroner James Beyer's autopsy, as do the several expert witness pathologists who render opinions of suicide. None of them examined the body but Beyer. In fact, it didn't take a massive conspiracy but rather only one doctor.

Reed Irvine

So what did Beyer's x-rays reveal? Patrick, John and Hugh got their answer from the Senate hearings. Lauch Faircloth was the only senator to ask the coroner tough questions:

SENATOR FAIRCLOTH: Dr. Beyer, your autopsy report indicates that you took x-rays of Mr. Foster.

Dr. BEYER: I had anticipated taking them, and I had so stated on one of my reports.

SENATOR FAIRCLOTH: Your autopsy report says you took x-rays of Mr. Foster. Did you?

Dr. BEYER: No, sir.

SENATOR FAIRCLOTH: Why did you say you did if you didn't?

DR. JAMES BEYER
DEPUTY MEDICAL EXAMINER
Northern Virginia

C-SPAN
FRI.

Dr. BEYER: As I indicated, I made out that report prior to actually performing the autopsy. We'd been having difficulty with our equipment, and we were not getting readable x-rays. Therefore, one was not taken.

SENATOR FAIRCLOTH: What was wrong with the x-ray machine?

Dr. BEYER: We had a new machine; we had new grids; and we had a new processor. We were having a number of problems.

SENATOR FAIRCLOTH: Why didn't you call Fairfax Hospital and arrange for a portable x-ray machine to be brought in for your use in such an important occasion?

Dr. BEYER: Because this was a perforating gunshot wound. If it had been a penetrating one, I would have gotten an x-ray of the head.

This jargon made little sense, and the senator was not deterred.

SENATOR FAIRCLOTH: Did you or the Medical Examiner's office have your servicing company come in and fix the x-ray machine?

Dr. BEYER: We were trying to remedy our problems. At that particular time we were not getting readable x-rays.

SENATOR FAIRCLOTH: When was it repaired?

Dr. BEYER: I have no x-rays in my files between July 6 to the 26. After July 26, 1993, we were getting x-rays.

SENATOR FAIRCLOTH: You mean for 20 days you ran a coroner's office and did autopsies without an x-ray machine?

Dr. BEYER: We don't take x-rays on very many cases. Primarily only gunshot cases.

Reed Irvine checked into this story and recorded his conversation with Jesse Poore, who serviced Beyer's x-ray equipment. Poore said he received no service calls from Beyer's office until October, three months after Foster's death.

Senator Faircloth was miffed by a statement in an early Park Police report which notes, "Dr. Beyer stated that x-rays indicated there was no evidence of bullet fragments in the head."[90]

SEN. LAUCH FAIRCLOTH
R-NORTH CAROLINA
C-SPAN
TODAY

SENATOR FAIRCLOTH: The Park Police officers who were present at the autopsy said you told them not only was an x-ray taken, you also told them the results of the x-ray. How do you account for the contradiction?

Dr. BEYER: I have no explanation because I did not take an x-ray.

SENATOR FAIRCLOTH: How did you tell the Park Police the results of an x-ray that you didn't take?

Dr. BEYER: I don't recall telling --

SENATOR FAIRCLOTH: Well, they do.

Dr. BEYER: I have no explanation.[91]

It was not the only time that Beyer, who contracted extensively with the government, had rendered a suicide verdict under strange circumstances. Patrick's team found the example of Tommy Burkett from the newspapers. He was found in his parents home with a revolver in his hand and, like Foster, Beyer ruled his death a suicide. The autopsy report cited a wound from mouth through the head with no signs of struggle.

But the parents received reports that their son was a DEA informant and that the suspected killer was the son of a DEA official. They commissioned a second autopsy which showed Tommy's ear had suffered trauma, his jaw had been broken, and abrasions were on his chest. Like with Foster, Beyer said he took no x-rays and also failed to dissect his lungs, though the report said he did.[92] "Beyer is nothing but a stooge for the FBI," said the boy's parents, in an open letter to the public.[93]

The case of Timothy Easley was much cleaner. He had been stabbed in the chest, but the parents did not believe Beyer's ruling of suicide. Photographs showed cut marks on the back of his hand, classic defense wounds. Experts contradicted Beyer again, but those opinions proved unnecessary. Easley's girlfriend confessed to the murder.[94]

Paramedic at the Foster scene, Richard Arthur, also ignored Beyer's single-testimony allegations. Arthur saw no exit wound at the back of Foster's head. He saw a bullet wound on the neck. "Fine, whether the coroner's report says that or not, fine. I know what I saw," he told a senate committee.[95]

10.

Although the marriage was deeply damaged, it would be wrong to say Hillary and Bill did not kindle a remaining connection. Bill still held a strong emotional power over Hillary. Once the antidote to her ungrateful father, Bill now performed a similar role of elusive affirmation. Hillary could not quite be as good as the other women in Bill's life. Instead of quitting, she kept striving to win his full affection, once again through performance and achievement and problem solving. While "fixing" an affair if it become dangerous served Hillary's political ambitions, it was also another way to win Bill's appreciation.

She had plenty of opportunities to perform this service as Bill's bid for the Presidency neared the 1992 Democrat Convention.

Dolly Kyle Browning was a longtime Clinton lover who likely had angered Hillary on a personal level with her novel about an affair with a Governor. "Mallory," the governor's wife, was "dowdy-looking" and an embarrassment. "She was wearing a mishapen brown dress that must have been intended to hide her lumpy body" but didn't cover "her fat ankles and thick calves."[96] This description of the Governor's wife included sandals, greasy hair, and glasses with Coke-bottle lenses, all appropriate descriptions of hippy Hillary when Browning first started seeing Clinton in the late seventies.

According to Browning, someone warned her to keep her mouth shut. She obliged.[97]

Dolly Kyle Browning

Elizabeth Ward Gracen, later to become famous for her role in the "Highlander" TV series, had also just been featured in *Playboy*. Evidence of an affair with Clinton would be dynamite for the media. She agreed to make a statement that the rumors were false.[98]

Former Miss Arkansas Sally Perdue was now working as a reporter for the local public TV station. Troopers relayed stories of how they would park the limousine a good distance from Perdue's condo and wait several hours until the porch light flickered—their cue to pick up the Governor. Perdue had already taped a segment with the *Sally Jesse Raphael* show," scheduled during the Democrat Convention, but it never aired.[99]

The most famous of the "Bimbo Eruptions," as Betsy Wright dubbed them to the *Washington Post*, was Gennifer Flowers. Shapely and talented, Flowers met Clinton in 1977 as a reporter for KARK TV and later took a job as a nightclub singer. Some liaisons occurred during Bill's morning runs.[100] When he passed her second floor condo, she would rush downstairs to open the side utility door. Other times they met for hours in the evenings, and the sordid details are described in later books by Flowers.

Hillary knew about her. Flowers was hired to sing at an event on the grounds of the Governor's mansion. Hillary cut her a furious look and walked off, but Gennifer says Bill attempted to take her to a first floor bathroom and lock the door behind them. Another time, Hillary came upon Bill chatting with Gennifer at a fundraiser. "I'm headed to the bar, Bill. Come join me," she said. "No, you go ahead," Bill answered while Flowers exulted in her little victory.[101]

Flowers says Clinton impregnated her in 1979 and paid for an abortion.[102] A decade later when reporters were on the warpath for bimbo eruptions, she lost her job as the paparazzi descended on the nightclub. She turned to Bill for help. Gennifer soon had a state job for which she was not qualified.[103] Another employee filed a formal complaint. Bill and Gennifer later discussed how to handle it. These and earlier phone conversations were taped by Flowers. They included strategies on how to handle the press. "If they ever hit you with it, just say no and go on," said Bill. "There's nothing they can do. I expected them to look into it and come interview you. But if everybody is on record denying it, no problem."[104]

Gennifer Flowers

As Flower's hearing neared, threats also emerged. Twice she came home and the deadbolt was locked, though she hadn't left it that way. Another time, the door was simply left open and her condo had been ransacked. All her old photos had been sifted through. Clinton told her it was "Republican harassment," but she began to suspect the Clinton folks themselves.

Gennifer's neighbor, Attorney Gary Johnson, had a surveillance camera that taped the activity outside Flowers' front door. When word of it got out, Johnson was beaten severely, several bones broken. Gennifer's mother who lived in another state got a phone call from a stranger. Your daughter would be "better off dead," he told her.[105]

Who was responsible for such activity? The *Washington Post* reported that private investigator Jack Palladino had been hired by the Clinton campaign. A San Francisco legend, Palladino billed at $2000 a day. Betsy Wright told the *Post* that Palladino's job was to track down the bimbos, "to figure out where and why some of these charges [against Clinton] are being leveled."[106]

One day, Palladino had a conversation with Gennifer's roommate Loren Kirk. "Is Gennifer the kind of person to commit suicide?" he asked. The question scared both women.[107]

Dolly Kyle Browning later admitted that someone affiliated with the Clinton campaign had warned her to be silent or they would "destroy you."[108]

Revelations of Palladino's dirty tricks brought credibility to Sally Perdue's allegations a month after her *Sally Jesse Raphael* show was canceled. A man asked to meet with her at a local restaurant. Wary, Purdue had a friend sit nearby, who heard the man warn her to keep her mouth shut and then threaten her. "He couldn't guarantee what might happen to my pretty little legs," she said.[109]

When Gennifer Flowers went public with her story about an affair with Clinton, the routine plan to deny, deny, deny worked. But the media exploded upon the release of Gennifer's tapes. While not proving an affair, they suggest deep intimacy. Flowers relayed a mock interview with a friend:

Flowers: "I said, 'You eat good pussy.'"

Clinton: "What!"

Sally Perdue

Flowers: (laughing) "I said, 'I had to tell them you ate good pussy,' and you said, 'Well, you can tell them that if I don't run for President.'"

The tapes also record Clinton urging Flowers to lie about how she got her job as well as his overall coaching to deny everything.[110]

Tape recordings threw a huge wrench in the strategy of blanket denial. Campaign operatives quickly sought to examine the tapes. Dick Morris strongly insinuates the campaign hired Anthony Pellicano, later exposed for threatening reporters and then being arrested by the FBI for possessing hand grenades and other explosives.[111]

Press releases soon proclaimed the tapes to be doctored. It wasn't enough. The nation needed to know what Clinton's wife believed. With the primary election hanging in the balance, the entire nation was watching on Sunday night after the Super Bowl as Bill and Hillary were interviewed on *60 Minutes.*

When asked about Flower's insistence of an affair, Bill Clinton denied it: "That allegation is false." Interviewer Steve Kroft wanted to make it perfectly clear, asking if he categorically denied her accusations of an affair.

"I've said that before, and so has she," Bill said.

The audience expected this from Clinton. They wanted to hear from Hillary.

"There isn't a person watching this who would feel comfortable sitting here on this couch detailing everything that ever went on in life or their marriage," she told Kroft. "And I think it's real dangerous in this country if we don't have some zone of privacy for everyone . . ."[112]

People got the message. There was probably something going on with Bill and Gennifer, but Hillary was not letting it ruin the marriage. She was moving on. So could they. But one more comment proved to haunt the future First Lady. "You know, I'm not sitting here—some little woman standing by my man like Tammy Wynette. I'm sitting here because I love him, and I honor what we've been through together. And if that's not enough for people, then heck, don't vote for him."[113]

The Clintons discuss Gennifer Flowers on 60 Minutes

The truth is, she was acting exactly like Tammy Wynette. Nevertheless, her performance on *60 Minutes* proved to be the campaign's turning point. The Clintons were elected to the White House, proving the Clintons' recorded motto to be more than effective: "If everyone is on record denying it, no problem."[114]

11.

As more powerful evidence was being gathered by the Knowlton trio, troubling information emerged showing that Patrick's bashed up Peugeot was no coincidence. At the time, Patrick had not connected it to his second FBI interview the following day. But a retired police captain, Rufus Peckham, had witnessed the man with the crowbar, and was savvy enough to write down the man's license plate. The Illinois Oldsmobile tracked to a Ronald Houston. The Justice Department looked into it, and learned that it was Houston's brother-in-law, Scott Jeffrey Bickett, who had committed the crime. Caught red-handed by the retired police captain, Bickett confessed to the crime, but the Justice Department did nothing. "It was just a dispute over a parking space," said prosecutor Mary McClaren.[115]

Ambrose had connections with database experts. Bickett, in fact, worked for the Pentagon, and his credentials were public record. They included "FBI-HQ," meaning he sometimes worked for the FBI, as well as "Active SCI," which stands for Sensitive Compartmented Information. It is the highest clearance offered by the U.S. Government, higher than Top Secret.[116]

Like the redactions, this revelation made them all wonder what forces were behind the harassment of a simple witness of a death scene. It was one thing to be stared at by strange men on the street. But Patrick realized he was now physically threatened by secret, sinister forces. His life may be in danger.

This could have been enough to cause Patrick to back down, but more positive news had emerged. Fiske, who had only given his "preliminary report," had been ousted. The Senate Banking Committee had accepted his ruling of suicide, but the financial side of Whitewater was causing a demand for a more independent investigation. He lost the position of top Whitewater investigator to another high-profile Republican: Kenneth E. Starr.

Fiske had the problem of looking like "the fox guarding the hen house." He was appointed by the official who oversees the FBI, Attorney General Janet Reno. She was appointed by the President. Like in Watergate, such inside investigations are usually followed by a cry for an independent probe—independent of the executive branch. After Watergate, Congress enacted the Office of Independent Counsel (or OIC) to investigate Presidents and their police powers.

When the OIC was cranked up again for Whitewater and Fostergate, the independent head honcho was, by definition, not appointed by the President. A panel of three top Federal judges from the U.S. Court of Appeals got this honor. Counting on a Beltway "go along, get along" mentality, Reno and Clinton expected Fiske to be re-appointed by the three judges. He would now be independent because he couldn't be fired by Clinton the way Nixon had fired his special prosecutor. The Foster case, already decided, would stand. Things would be fine.

Instead, the three-judge panel appointed Starr, someone they knew personally—a colleague on the bench and a well-known conservative. Starr was a past prosecutor under George H.W. Bush and made a million a year as a private attorney. He taught Sunday School to fourth graders. He held pro-family positions across the board. His appointment caused a media stir in the Beltway. Things were about to get interesting.

Ken Starr

Starr would not do the investigating himself. With a staff of hundreds, he served more like a chairman of the board. His top staff of bureaucrats which oversees a handful of prosecutors, calls secret grand juries to grill witnesses, leading possibly to criminal indictments. Ultimately, his team is required to submit a comprehensive Final Report to the three judge panel that appointed Starr with hundreds of pages of documentation, providing a final word on the matter for history. The legislative and judicial branches therefore keep a healthy check on the executive branch. The OIC protects us from fascism. We have a Constitution, not a king.

The many Americans suspicious of the Whitewater scandal and Foster "suicide" were hopeful that Ken Starr would get to the bottom of it. But would his staff be as unreliable as Fiske's?

Patrick was also hopeful Starr would make a difference. But while Starr investigated on behalf of the legislative branch, Patrick's lawsuit pitched the judiciary against President Clinton. However, this also proved to be a difficult effort. The District Court of Washington D.C. decided not to hear his case. To Patrick's amazement, they said there was not enough evidence to warrant a hearing. The only recourse was to appeal the case, and Patrick's cause was soon to be reviewed by the United States Supreme Court, if they chose to hear it.

Unfortunately, foreboding news began to leak in the Beltway. Leaks to the press are a way of life in Washington, and they are usually accurate, preceding the coming formality. The Foster death had already been determined by Starr's investigation, the press said, citing anonymous sources. It was a suicide, pure and simple.

But that's not what Reed Irvine found out. He taped all of his phone calls, and he had been carrying on secret phone conversations with Starr's prosecutor, Miguel Rodriguez, and the reports were exciting. The top prosecutor for the OIC's Foster investigation was taking the bull by the horns and grilling the key witnesses before a grand jury. The leak to the press had been premature. In fact, it was intended as sabotage.[117] Starr's office had not concluded the case. Rather, there was a war going on in the Office of Independent Counsel.

12.

Miguel Rodriguez was chosen for the task as top prosecutor of the Foster affair while serving as an Assistant District Attorney in Sacramento. Hispanic and slight of build, the Harvard graduate sported an earring and wore various leather jackets. Those hoping for a hardnosed interrogator felt this West Coast ethnic liberal was just another attempt to make the OIC look diverse and tolerant.[118] It was rumored that Rodriguez was gay. In fact, some thought closeted gays were recruited for such posts. Easier to control.

None of the stereotyping succeeded. Miguel was determined to crack the case. He told Reed Irvine during their clandestine phone calls that he was not like Fiske.

Miguel Rodriguez: "Fiske himself indicated that he had determined the result before he had ever released a report. The results, you know, were dictated, and I don't do that kind of work."[119]

Unfortunately, Miguel's superior, Mark Tuohey III, did not see it that way. The number two man under Starr, Tuohey was not a prosecutor but a politically active bureaucrat, and a Democrat. He pulled Miguel aside early on. It would be ill-advised to challenge Fiske's initial findings, he said.[120]

Tuohey wasn't just your run-of-the-mill Democrat. His wife was Marty Daley—he married into the Daley political machine of Chicago. The infamous Mayor Richard J. Daley was Tuohey's father-in-law. Daley's son, Tuohey's brother-in-law, was also a Chicago Mayor.

The Daleys are considered to be one of the most corrupt political families in American history. According to NBC: "Robert Sorich, Daley's patronage chief, was convicted in 2006 for rewarding the mayor's political allies with city jobs and promotions ... His father, the late Mayor Richard J. Daley, built the once-mighty machine that doled out jobs and favors in exchange for support for Democrats on Election Day. He was never charged with criminal wrongdoing, but several of his high-ranking aides were sent to prison for political patronage."[121]

Miguel Rodriguez

Unlike Tuohey, Miguel was not political. He was a prosecutor. He didn't know how else to operate. He started calling key witnesses to the grand jury. His findings were strongly corroborating the evidence and theories unraveled by Patrick, John, and Hugh.

Miguel: "There is no evidence that that gun was ever found to have ever been part of the family. It contradicts an earlier statement by (his wife) Lisa that it wasn't the gun."[122]

He also told Reed the type of gun had changed at the scene.

Miguel: "Even the Park Police and the person who first saw the body saw different things. But there was a point in time where the particular gun that he described arrived and something before that was either not observed or not completely identified."[123]

He was talking about the automatic pistol which Paramedic Richard Arthur had first identified, the same medic who stuck to his story about a bullet wound in the neck, despite being warned not to talk.

Miguel was also aware of the testimony of Arthur's partner, Todd Hall. When Hall approached Foster's body, he saw men running away from the scene into the woods.[124] After several FBI interviews, Hall conceded it could have possibly been cars on the highway that he saw.[125]

Miguel admired both Arthur and Todd's testimony:

Miguel: "Both EMTs that responded to the Park both observed trauma to the neck. While Arthur remained clear on it despite the FBI's attempt to shake him, the other one was confused by the FBI and kept saying what he saw but they kept writing it a different way."[126]

When Miguel brought Hall before the grand jury, he asked Hall if he saw cars or people running from the body scene. It could have been cars, but what he saw was people.[127]

Miguel had no doubt about the bullet hole the two medics had seen.

Miguel: "I saw pictures that clearly indicate to me that there is trauma on the neck. I believe it's a puncture wound on the neck."[128]

The FBI and certain staff at the OIC were not happy with where Miguel Rodriguez was headed.

Miguel: "They told me, to quote, this is a quote: 'Back off.' It was either 'back off' or 'back down.' They used both."[129]

But Miguel kept asking tough questions. He told Reed he knew all about Patrick Knowlton, the problem of the car, and his harassment by the FBI.

Miguel: "What does this guy Knowlton have to gain by saying something that he said from the outset—and continues to say today? Why is the FBI harassing and re-interviewing witnesses who have no incentive to lie? And yet, we are treating with rubber gloves persons who do have an incentive to lie! Knowlton should find comfort in the fact that he is not alone. He needs to know that. The guy is a damn hero."[130]

13.

Normally, the First Lady operates from her office in the East Wing of the White House. Hillary insisted on an office in the West Wing. At first she demanded the Vice President's office, but Al Gore refused. She ended up with West Wing offices just next to the White House Counsel, where Vince Foster worked. [131]

By most accounts, Hillary was actively involved in running the country. Within days, Hillary's staff had a banner that proclaimed, "Hillary for President."[132]

Appointing cabinet members caused immediate controversy nationwide. Hillary was known to be behind the strange characters, and Vince was charged with vetting her choices. Lani Guineer was outed as a Socialist while Roberta Achtenberg's vehement activism for lesbian rights infuriated conservative America. Always nutty Joycelyn Elders was later removed as Surgeon General for advocating masturbation.[133]

Hillary's first two choices for Attorney General were rejected by the Senate, both cited for using illegal nannies. Bill Clinton could have avoided much grief during these early days of his presidency by picking safer nominees, but many believed he had conceded this major task to Hillary in exchange for her "60 Minutes" performance. Hillary got what she wanted, and she likely was not happy with Vince when the vetting process failed.

Foster followed the Clintons to the White House

Bill and Hillary made the White House a different place. Tradition made way for the progressive. Casual clothes and late night office trysts replaced suits and formal dinners by a gourmet French chef. Hillary pushed for lighter portions. She also replaced the traditional decorations and hired her longtime friend Kaki to redo the mansion.

Christmastime brought new ideas for decoration. The tree showcased two turtledoves mating, three French hens in a threesome, five golden rings on a gingerbread man's ear, nipple, navel, nose, and penis, and twelve excited and erect Lords-a-Leaping .[134]

Other ornaments were made of drug paraphernalia such as syringes and roach clips.[135] In fact, hundreds of White House employees had not passed their drug tests. One method of bypassing this problem involved the key position of Director of White House Management and Administration, the overseer of drug testing. For this post, Hillary chose personal confidante Patsy Thomasson.[136] In Arkansas, she was top assistant to major Clinton donor Dan Lasatar, convicted for social distribution of cocaine. While Lasatar was in jail, Patsy ran the company.[137]

Hillary ran the White House with a confident and clear mission: there is no substitute for victory—attack the enemy, protect the good guys at all cost. Vince Foster was at the center of Hillary's command structure. No doubt, the growing list of Clinton scandals was building stress for him personally and damaging his relationship with Hillary herself.

At one point, Clinton staffers were given a memo listing the dozen or so scandals and how to deal with them. Hillary's secretive healthcare initiative was being challenged in the courts, the press was asking hard questions about the firing of seven travel office employees who were later investigated by the FBI and IRS. They were all innocent: were they fired to make way for Hillary's friends? Controversy had even erupted over the funds for redecorating the White House, and Hillary was charged with going way over budget.[138]

Whitewater was not yet a household word, but Vince Foster knew all about it, more than anyone else, including, possibly, the Clintons. He was years late in filing the tax returns for Whitewater and was also dragging his feet in putting the Clinton's assets in a blind trust, an action that required his signing under oath that everything in the trust was true and accurate. Several months had passed. All previous administrations filed their blind trust before inauguration day.

"Fix it, Vince!"[139] was a directive overheard by White House staffers when Hillary's problems heated up. Vince got it from both sides. The *Wall Street Journal* wrote several editorials about his secretive ways and the suspicious activities behind the Travelgate scandal.

The third week of July was a busy one. On Wednesday, Senate Majority Leader Bob Dole called for an investigation into the Travelgate scandal.[140] If Vince was involved in siccing the IRS and FBI on the innocent travel staff, he may have to testify about it under oath. A few days later, a subpoena was issued to a judge in Little Rock closely related to the Whitewater scandal.[141]

On Friday, Vince and his wife Lisa headed to a remote hotel on the Eastern Shore of Maryland. But soon enough, they were tracked down by old friend Webb Hubbell, one of the "three amigos," as they called themselves, with Hillary and Vince at the Rose Law Firm back in Little Rock. He invited Vince and Lisa to join them at a nearby estate owned by his friend, Nathan Landow. Lisa enjoyed the various activities made available, including tennis lessons from Pam Shriver, while Vince and the men talked. Webb testified later that their time together was relaxed and leisurely.[142] Lisa said of the weekend, "It had not gone particularly well."[143]

Regardless, the following Monday at work, many people seemed to be interested in the discussions over the weekend. Webb Hubbell stopped in twice to talk to Vince. Another Little Rock crony, William Kennedy, called twice. Marsha Scott, the White House Director of Correspondence and a confidante of Bill's, walked over in the afternoon from the Old Executive Office Building for a closed door meeting.[144] It lasted two hours, an unusually long time, said Linda Tripp,[145] who worked in Foster's office before moving later to the Pentagon and meeting Monica Lewinsky. While Tripp was leaving the office, Marsha Scott asked Vince, "If I see Bill before you do, what do you want me to tell him?"[146]

Webb Hubbell

That evening, Clinton called Foster at his home. The conversation lasted fifteen minutes. Clinton later testified that he asked Vince to come up and watch a movie at the White House—Clint Eastwood's "In the Line of Fire"—but Vince declined.[147]

The next day was Vince Foster's last. He drove his kids to their workplaces—or so we are told—and eventually was working at his office that morning.[148] His assistant said he was working on a memo about the Waco disaster.[149] At 1:00 pm, after Linda Tripp had gotten him a sandwich which he ate in his office, Foster offered Tripp some M&Ms, said he would be back, and walked away.[150] He was last seen by the downstairs Secret Service agent as Foster walked to the parking lot or perhaps to the Old Executive Office Building across the street, where Bill Kennedy and Marsha Scott worked.[151]

Hillary says she only spoke to Vince once during the month before his death. "Well, you know, the last specific conversation I can recall is this phone conversation which was either Friday or Saturday before Father's Day, whatever that was, I guess it was like mid-June," Hillary stated under oath. "He said, well, why don't you come out to dinner with us . . . I just couldn't do it because I had too much else to do. And that's all."[152]

But a staffer in the White House Counsel's office testified otherwise. Thomas Castleton, a colleague of Foster and Tripp's, worked in the West Wing. Like Tripp, he saw Foster leave at 1:00 pm on Tuesday, July 20. He had only started working in the White House Counsel's office on June 16, four days before Father's Day. His FBI 302 cites several meetings between Vince and Hillary. "He said that he saw Hillary Clinton in Vincent Foster's office approximately four times,"[153] reads the FBI report, which was not made public for several years. (Patrick and Hugh found it in the National Archives.)[154]

Marsha Scott, tall, blonde, athletic, and long known to be one of Bill Clinton's paramours, was apparently rewarded with Clinton's bed the night of Foster's death. She was "pretty pumped up about the whole thing," said Eileen Watkins, tennis partner of Lisa Foster and wife of White House Director of Administration, David Watkins. "She told me, 'I spent the night in his bed. I had my head in his lap, and we reminisced all night long.'"[155]

14.

Inside the Office of Independent Counsel, one of the main rivals for Miguel Rodriguez was young prosecutor Brett Kavanaugh. He resisted the idea that Foster did not drive his gray Honda to the park that day. Reed called Kavanaugh. What evidence do you have for a gray car, he asked.

Kavanaugh: "The question is whether there is evidence, other than no one saw it being moved out, and, you know, it had Arkansas plates."

Reed: "But all these witnesses saw a brown car, not a gray one."

Kavanaugh: "What about the people who seemed to clearly see Foster's car, and described it as brown?"

Reed: "Maybe it wasn't Foster's car."

Kavanaugh: "People were screwed up on the colors, period."[156]

Brett Kavanaugh

Miguel (from another recording): "It's not just Tuohey. There's a lot of people that are, are very interested in controlling the result here—the young aspiring people, you know, who will, will say and do what they have to, to move up the ladder."[157]

Miguel continued to grill Park Police officers, particularly on the many photographs at the scene, most of them lost. After many contradictions emerged, Miguel felt compelled to read the perjury statute to each of them in a deliberate manner.[158]

The first officer to take photos, Franz Ferstl, said his seven polaroids were snatched up by a superior at the body scene. They were never seen again.[159] Detective John Rolla took a number of photos that were lost. "I mean, I had them in the office that night, I did reports, and I don't know what happened," he testified in Senate Depositions. "I put them in a jacket, I don't know."[160]

The official photographer for the scene was Park Police technician Pete Simonello. His entire roll of 35 mm photos was declared "underexposed" by the FBI. He was surprised. His camera has never failed before or since.[161] Even more strange, medic Arthur was shown a blow up of one of Simonello's photos during his FBI interview. "They appeared to be pretty clear," he said.[162] They even showed a few of them to Simonello himself who said they "looked good to me. They didn't look underexposed."[163]

Miguel: "I think that the photographs that were taken for several people don't exist any longer or they have never been turned over to reviewing officials. At least seven were missing, and that was established at one point. I had a person look at 13 photographs and that person told me, 'Mine are not here.'"[164]

What in the world was going on in the Park that night? Miguel was determined to get to the bottom of it. But Patrick's team had already figured out a great deal without the help of a grand jury. Poring through a myriad of reports, interviews, and depositions, and thousands of Senate documents, a clearer sense of who arrived first, second, third, etc. began to emerge.

The original 911 call no longer exists. A second one is available, but sounds staged, as might be expected.[165] There is confusion as to who first reported a body in the park and made the 911 call, and some versions say a private citizen found Foster with no gun in his hand. This witness left the body, reported it to Park Service workers, and drove away.[166]

But the first official to find the body was Park Police Officer Kevin Fornshill. The park wasn't part of his responsibility; his job was to guard the entrance to the CIA, a stone's throw from Fort Marcy Park. He heard the report on his radio and speedily headed to the scene.[167]

Fornshill was not interviewed for a year.[168] In fact, he says none of his colleagues even asked him anything about what he saw, according to his Senate deposition:

Q. Did any of the detectives on the scene come and talk to you?

A. No...

Q. None of these guys ever talked to you about the crime scene?

A. No, not that I know of.[169]

Fornshill arrived at the parking lot at the same time as two medics, Todd Hall and George Gonzales. He suggested the two of them search for the body up to the left. He headed the other direction and was savvy enough to find the Foster body immediately.[170] He called to the medics and Hall arrived first. Hall told Fornshill he saw men running away, but Fornshill did not respond.[171]

Gonzales then arrived and viewed the body.[172] Next arriving was Franz Ferstl, the Park Police beat officer who ordinarily would have been first on the scene, had Fornshill not arrived earlier. The two medics left, others arrived such as Richard Arthur (who saw the bullet wound in the neck). Ferstl left to get his camera. When he returned, he took seven polaroid pictures of Foster with a gun—identified by Arthur as an automatic, not a revolver.

As Ferstl was snapping pictures, Sgt. Bob Edwards arrived and took charge of the scene. The other Park Police officers were not familiar with him. "I didn't know who this guy was. Nobody [knew] who this guy was," said Detective Rolla, who arrived a few minutes after Edwards and took over.[173]

But several minutes before Rolla walked up to the body scene, Edwards gave directions. Ferstl was there with Fornshill, who had been alone with the body several minutes early on. Edwards told Fornshill to go back and guard the CIA entrance. He then took Ferstl's seven polaroids and ordered him to return to the parking lot.[174]

When Rolla arrived, Edwards was alone and was taking polaroid pictures of Foster, who was now holding a .38 caliber revolver.[175] (Miguel believed it had likely been planted just before or upon Rolla's arrival.[176]) The neck wound was now partially covered by accounts of a blood spill,[177] fresh blood which several did not see who arrived earliest at the body scene.[178] Rolla and partner Cheryl Braun took charge of the scene, and Edwards returned to the parking lot and left.

Park Police technician Pete Simonello's photos were "underexposed."

Sgt. Bob Edwards was never mentioned by the FBI or Robert Fiske. The Senate never took his deposition. The first officer in command at Vince Foster's death scene was interviewed years later by the Starr Investigation. It remains secret.[179]

The secrecy angers Rodriguez.

Miguel: "God! I'm just brimming over, I'm bubbling over. And I'm angry that I cannot respond. Because there is much to be said. What background did they have? Wouldn't it be surprising if these people were special liaisons in a prior life? And have you really identified all the main players out there at the Park Police?"[180]

One player involved does have a strange background— Jim Clemente, Supervisory Special Agent for the FBI's Behavior Analysis Unit, and today a nationally recognized expert in Sex Crimes Investigation, Sex Offender Behavior, Child Sexual Victimization, and Child Pornography. Clemente was a key FBI agent on staff with the Starr Investigation, and spent many hours questioning Patrick Knowlton.

Years later, Knowlton and Turley found a strange document in the National Archives, a cover page for a report that was not included in the box of records made available to the public. The report is entitled: "Child Abduction and Serial Killer Unit: Questions for a Suicide Expert; Vince Foster Death Investigation."[181]

No one knows what it means.

15.

Ted Koppel (on TV): "Even suppose some covered things up. How do you get all the others to conspire?"[182]

Miguel (on audio tape): "Everyone makes a very big mistake when they believe that a lot of people are necessary to orchestrate some kind of—some result here. All you need to do is just have a couple of people involved. Very few people need to know anything about anything, really. All people need to know is what their job is, not why. Be a good soldier, carry out orders. When you write a report, all you have to do is make sure it's consistent . . . consistent with the result that you ultimately want to get, which is to not embarrass your other colleagues who have made their conclusions already."[183]

Miguel Rodriguez determined one major reason why certain interviews were not being conducted and others were constantly twisted. The common link was the same handful of investigating FBI agents. They helped in the Park Police's initial investigation, in what amounted to a joint effort. They then conducted follow up interviews, ran the Fiske investigation and were now conducting the investigative duties for Starr. The same agency controlled the witnesses, the documents, and the evidence.[184] Now, Starr was letting them investigate their own work.

Miguel: "I said, 'Look, I think it might be a good idea to use different FBI agents.' They went through the roof!

They went absolutely nuts! They had everything the way they wanted it."[185]

Of the 18 photographs that remain, none of them show Foster's head and neck. A famous photograph released by ABC shows the gun,[186] but no photos exist to prove the gun was held by Foster. Other photos show close ups of the gray car, a briefcase, the eyeglasses and other items with limited value.[187]

Thanks to an insider at the FBI lab, Miguel obtained a photo that clearly showed the neck wound caused by a bullet. It was locked away, deliberately withheld from the key prosecutor.[188]

Miguel: "I had to go through great lengths to get it and I had to do it myself."[189]

Initially, he had viewed the doctored, third generation version. The neck wound had been smeared to look like a blood stain.[190]

Miguel: "That was a Polaroid, a picture of a picture of a picture. There were three layers. It was third generation. The first, the whole team of forensic scientists looked at the third generation photographs, absolutely ridiculous."[191]

Dr. CHARLES HIRSCH (Senate Hearings): It is my unequivocal, categorical opinion, that it was impossible for him to be killed elsewhere.

SEN. FAIRCLOTH: . . . Were you present at the Foster autopsy?

Dr. HIRSCH: No, sir.

SEN. FAIRCLOTH: Have you actually examined the gun which was identified as the suicide weapon?

Dr. HIRSCH: No, sir.

SEN. FAIRCLOTH: Have you actually examined any other physical evidence?

Dr. HIRSCH: Let me go back to the question of the gun. I haven't had the gun physically in my hands. I've seen photographs of it . . .

SEN. FAIRCLOTH: Have you interviewed anyone in the case other than Dr. Beyer?

Dr. HIRSCH: I didn't personally interview Dr. Beyer.[192]

Unlike the various experts and panelists, Miguel was examining the primary evidence. With the help of grand jury testimony from Park Police officers, Miguel was proceeding toward breaking the cover-up. One Park Police Officer had already confessed in secret grand jury testimony that the crime scene had been altered.[193] But the bureaucrats at Starr's Office of Independent Counsel blocked Miguel's every turn.

Miguel: "I was unable to call witnesses and issue subpoenas, and, under control of the Democrat Mark Tuohey, . . . compromised. My office was searched by him, you know. I know what he is capable of doing. That includes throwing tantrums and throwing chairs."[194]

Handwritten notes on a private meeting between Starr's #3 man Hickman Ewing and Rodriguez reveal the severity of Mark Tuohey's opposition.

Ewing reported that Rodriguez said "Mark Tuohey threatened him professionally" and is "fighting the truth."

According to the notes, Rodriguez's administrative assistant was also "terrorized by Mark Tuohey" and asked her to "lie about Miguel Rodriguez."[195]

16.

A year after Bill Clinton was elected, Christy Zircher was contacted by the *Washington Post*. She told the reporter about Clinton's many advances toward her as a flight attendant on the Clinton Campaign jet, Longhorn One. Clinton discussed with her Gennifer Flowers' claims of his excellent sexual techniques in her *Star* tabloid interview and told Christy, "That's about right."

Once, he dipped his finger in his tea and sucked on it, mimicking oral sex, and invited her into the plane's lavatory. On another occasion, Hillary was on board. While she slept, Clinton crept over to the seat beside Christy and started stroking her chest. Afraid of causing a scene and waking Hillary, Christy did nothing.

But a few days after her talks with the reporter, Christy's house was burglarized at 2 am while she slept upstairs. No jewelry was taken, only her diary and most of her photographs. Christy got the message and stopped talking to the *Post*, which never wrote the story.[196]

But a girl from Little Rock was more difficult. Paula Jones was implicated by the state police officers of enjoying a tryst with Clinton after troopers left them sitting on a couch in a hotel suite. She filed suit against the President demanding an apology. According to Paula, she resisted his advances, and left the scene after Clinton dropped his pants and said, "Kiss it."[197]

Paula Jones

Jones had started a legal fund and her attorneys were making progress and naming other women. Clinton's attorney Robert Bennett urged the President to settle with Jones for a small amount of money and a vague apology. But Hillary refused. Bennett was surprised, but had not been long acquainted with the First Lady, whose first instinct was always to deny and attack.[198]

One of the women named was Elizabeth Ward Gracen, the former Miss America who years before had agreed to make a statement that she had never had an affair with Bill Clinton. When Gracen was warned to duck subpoenas coming her way from the Jones legal team, she headed to a resort in the Carribbean. But after her room was ransacked, she decided she could not trust either side and hired her own pricey attorney. She appeared on NBC's *Dateline* and admitted to a single sexual encounter with Clinton.[199]

Kathleen Willey was also named in the suit. Her friend Julia Steele told *Newsweek* that Kathleen had visited the Oval Office to ask her old friend Bill Clinton for a job.

Elizabeth Ward Gracen

Clinton groped her. Once again, Linda Tripp was a witness. She told *Newsweek* she saw Willey emerge from the Oval Office disheveled, as well as perhaps "joyful" for being the object of the President's affections. Willey refused to cooperate with the Jones attorneys, and was later appointed to an academic position in Indonesia.[200] When Willey's story re-emerged in the press, her house in Northern Virginia was burglarized. Her cats disappeared and her tires were slashed. A man jogged by her house, mentioned her tires and cats and asked if she got the message.[201]

The White House was eventually forced to reveal they had retained the services of Investigative Group International to track people accusing the President. In a deposition for a lawsuit by Judicial Watch, White House records director Terry W. Good admitted he had been ordered to search for "anything and everything we might have in our files on Linda Tripp."[202]

Clinton and Kathleen Willey

Judicial Watch also asked IGI's owner Terry Lenzner whether Hillary Clinton was a client, but Lenzner claimed privilege and refused to answer. One of Hillary's staffers, Brooke Shearer, worked previously for IGI. Raymond Kelly, another IGI man, had been made head of the White House Secret Service.[203] The position had been important to Hillary, who was furious over a secret service leak to the press on inauguration day. The First Lady was overheard calling Bill "you stupid motherfucker," while Bill responded with "you fucking bitch!" Other accounts included the throwing of lamps and furniture.[204]

Dick Morris, the former top strategist and confident of the Clintons for over a decade, called IGI the "White House secret police."[205] Noting that Shearer would rummage through dumpsters looking for damaging information, Morris makes it clear that the precedent is scary: "The use of detectives to scour the backgrounds of one's adversaries was not—and is not—common in American politics. Hillary and Bill were pioneers in this seamy pastime."[206]

Yet another woman emerged on the Jones attorney list, Monica Lewinsky. However, she willingly signed an affidavit saying she had no sexual contact whatever with President Clinton.[207]

Monica Lewinsky

The White House appealed to the Supreme Court to avoid being deposed by Jones's legal team, but lost. When the day came for several hours of grilling the President, he was confident. "He thought he could take care of the questions about Kathleen Willey and all the other women," said David Schippers, who oversaw the eventual impeachment hearings. "And he also felt that Monica was in the bag. He was smug, cocky, arrogant."[208]

Clinton used his same tried and true strategy: deny.

"Have you ever given any gifts to Monica Lewinsky?" he was asked.

"I don't recall."

"Did you ever have extramarital sex with Monica Lewinsky?"

"No."

The Jones attorneys expected as much that day, until they got to Gennifer Flowers.

"Did you ever have sexual relations with Gennifer Flowers?"

"Yes," Clinton replied.

"On how many occasions?"

"Once."[209]

The moment was a chink in the armor of the longtime Clinton strategy. Apparently, the legally trained Clinton knew the danger of lying under oath, and Flowers's charges were provable. But how did Jones's lawyers know so much about Monica, Clinton wondered. The bitter truth emerged when the press reported that, like with Gennifer Flowers, tapes could be the undoing of this President. Linda Tripp had emerged again, this time in the Pentagon, after moving there from the White House Counsel's office where Vince Foster once worked.

Tripp had befriended another Pentagon employee, Monica Lewinsky, and had learned all the sordid details of her affair with the President. When discussions turned to lying and false affidavits to protect the President, Tripp decided to tape the phone calls. Ultimately, she contacted Ken Starr's investigation with the evidence.

Linda Tripp

Starr was extremely interested. Starr's investigation had two centers: Washington, D.C. and Little Rock, Arkansas. In Little Rock, only David Hale was in jail, the small time judge who had plea-bargained to help Starr get the real criminals. Those bigger indictments never materialized. In Washington, not a single indictment had been handed down. Starr had little to show for several years and hundreds of staffers. Linda Tripp could change all that.

A few days after the Jones deposition, the news was blasting the rumors about Monica Lewinsky. Unlike Bill, Hillary had not wavered from the denial strategy. Once again, Hillary came to Bill's rescue about the Monica allegations: "If all that were proven true, I think that would be a very serious offense. This is not going to be proven true," Hillary said.[210]

93

Bill himself was back to the proven strategy: "Let me say this one time: I did not have sex with that woman, Miss Lewinsky," he said while looking into the camera at the American people.

17.

When it came time for Patrick to testify before Ken Starr's grand jury, the prosecutor was not Miguel Rodriguez, but rather his rival, Brett Kavanaugh.

Patrick sat at a table by himself in front of 12 grand jurors, mostly African-Americans, and the prosecutor stood to his right. Another prosecutor sat directly behind Patrick, which made him feel uncomfortable. No one can attend the secret proceedings except the court reporter. The witness cannot have his attorney present.[211]

Patrick had a bad feeling about the questioning. The prosecutor did not seem interested in the important details. He then asked Patrick about the "alleged harassment" he had received from nearly 30 men on the street.

"It was not alleged," said Patrick. "It happened."

Patrick Knowlton

He recounted the incident along with FBI Agent Bransford's disturbing follow up. "Who sent him to me?" Patrick asked.

"You don't need to know," the prosecutor replied.

Then the man behind him spoke for the first time. "We sent him," he said arrogantly.

That same man, named John Bates, then passed a note to the prosecutor, who asked Patrick more questions about the menacing man in the parking lot of Fort Marcy Park.

"Did the man talk to you?"

"No," Patrick replied.

"Did he pass you a note?"

"No."

"Did he point a gun at you?"

"No."

"Did he touch your genitals?"[212]

Patrick became visibly angry at the suggestion. The grand jurors were on Patrick's side. Nevertheless, the prosecutor kept badgering him.

"Are you a 'good citizen,' Mr. Knowlton?" Kavanaugh continued his bitter sarcasm. "Are you a 'good Samaritan'?"

It was one of the worst three hours of Patrick's life. Reed recounted the incident to Miguel:

Miguel: Who asked him if he touched his genitals?

Reed: Kavanaugh.

Miguel: How could Brett stoop so low? I can't believe Brett did that.[213]

Personally aware of such smear tactics, Miguel later explained to Reed what goes on inside the FBI and OIC.

Miguel: "What they are trying to do is discredit him by making him out to be, you know, a homosexual cruising at the park. I was literally irate with Tuohey and the FBI agents who were snickering and laughing with Brett about this. I don't care if they were fucking their favorite tree. And the FBI finds it particularly funny."

Patrick was worried. The OIC prosecutor had harassed him. Rodriguez himself was being harassed. Patrick was in debt nearly $100,000. John had sold his car to help pay the court costs.[214]

Incredibly, Patrick did not give up the fight. Anything he could uncover to help investigators like Miguel might be the one straw that breaks the camel's back of the cover-up. Regularly, he and Hugh would head to the National Archives and pore through hundreds of documents, hoping to find something.[215]

To his great pleasure, Patrick hit paydirt one day while combing through yet another box of papers. It was a report made the day of Foster's death which should have been released long before. The Senate Banking Committee never saw it. The one doctor to examine the body at the death scene, Medical Examiner Donald Haut, was never asked to hand over his report.

**Medical Examiner
Donald Haut**

Patrick, John and Hugh examined it. On the line where the wound is described, the typed words said: "Mouth to head." No surprise. But on further examination they could see tiny black dots to the left and above it. Something was clearly whited-out. The black marks on the bottom looked like the foundation for the word "neck." Typed instead, was the word "head."[216]

The person attempting to redact or forge or falsify this document did not realize more information on the wound was listed on the backside. There, Dr. Haut was crystal clear: "Gunshot, mouth to neck."[217]

It was another sizzling piece of evidence that corroborated all the research they had conducted before, as well as the findings of Miguel Rodriguez and the secret photo he had obtained.

However, lack of evidence was never the problem for Kenneth Starr and the Office of Independent Counsel. Miguel Rodriguez had uncovered a mountain of solid facts for an indictment. Miguel began to relay somber messages on the phone to Reed:

Miguel: "The Independent Counsel themselves, and the FBI, beat me back, and in fact threatened me. The Park Police were never asked tough questions. I tried to ask them tough questions and they beat the hell out of me. It was just bass ackwards."[218]

The life had been taken out of him, Reed thought. What was really going on, Miguel?

Miguel: "I have been communicated with again. And told to, you know, to be careful where I tread.[219]

He was being less than candid.

Miguel: "I can tell you this, that . . . that . . . it has not only to do with my career and reputation, um, they've also had to do with my personal health and family."

Miguel wasn't married. What exactly was he talking about?

Because of the serious problems, Miguel had taken the powerful evidence he had gathered to Ken Starr himself, and explained the harassment he received from his colleagues. Starr took it under advisement but did nothing.[220]

To document Starr's failure to pursue the truth, Rodriguez wrote a 30 page memo to "File," detailing the long list of facts that contradicted a suicide verdict—the problems with identifying the gun, the lack of a head wound, the missing x-rays, the neck wound identified by first responders, men seen in the woods running away from the corpse, the lack of fingerprints on the gun that had been "wiped clean" (except for one print underneath never identified), and the many lost or ruined photographs.

Miguel also noted that the four prints on the car were never identified, that at least four Park Police officers happened to arrive early on the scene "by coincidence," that foliage behind Foster's body in the pictures differed, and that Fort Marcy Park had private roads and parking lots in the other direction from the corpse. The Park Police officers knew about these secret roads but never discussed them.

The first witness saw no gun, but rather testified that Foster's hands were "palms up." Foster's semen was found on his shorts, and Miguel noted that semen is not released upon a fatal bullet to the head.

Rodriguez also spent several pages debunking a suicide motive, noting that recollections of depression only emerged after the fact, and nothing in the record before Foster's death indicates a problem. He quotes one of Foster's best friends who called him the morning of his death. "He was the same Vince I'd always known," said Gordan Rather. Foster's last words to his secretary upon leaving the office were, "I'll be back."[221]

Bitter news then emerged from the Office of Independent Counsel. Miguel Rodriguez, the lead prosecutor of the

Foster case, had resigned. In his resignation letter he listed again the many facts contradicting suicide. Although grand jury testimony "had been fruitful," his superiors informed him that "all planned grand jury investigation would be cancelled." Instead, wrote Miguel, "my own conduct was questioned, and I was placed under internal investigation ... I was to be more closely monitored by Tuohey and an FBI agent. In effect, for raising the above questions, I was forced out of a job."[222]

Reed asked him what happened:

Miguel: "I knew what the result was going to be, because I was told what the result was going to be from the get-go. That's why I left. I don't do investigations like that—do investigations to justify results. This whole notion, you know, of doing an honest investigation, you know, you know . . . it's laughable."[223]

Who was behind the corruption?

Miguel: "The result is being dictated by a lot higher, um, authority than I think people really understand or appreciate, and certainly more than I ever appreciated."[224]

Mark Tuohey III

Patrick was sickened. Would justice never triumph in this case, the highest suspicious death of a government official since JFK? Do the people, does the Congress elected by the people, have no check on the executive branch? Is the President now a dictator? Was Patrick's government, always known to him as promoter of liberty and truth worldwide and a provider and safety net at home, corrupt to its core?

His only remaining hope now was set on the judiciary, on his lawsuit, now hundreds of pages, filled with evidence such as the gun, the neck wound, the lack of an exit wound, and the missing photos and x-rays.

18.

Reports surfaced that IGI, the White House "secret police," was now investigating members of Starr's staff. *The Nation*, a left-wing publication, reported that Hillary's top aide Sid Blumenthal was spreading rumors that certain staff members for Starr investigator were gay.[225] Previously, Jim Leach, Chairman of the House Banking Committee, spotted a known Clinton private detective snooping around his house. Another burglar rifled through the car of Cheryl Mills as she was about to testify to a Senate Committee. According to a friend, they took Mills's notes on the handling of Vince Foster's papers at the time of his death.[226]

When the Starr investigation turned to Monica and the tapes of Linda Tripp, Hillary was clear about her position. "I do believe this is a battle," she told Matt Lauer on the *Today Show*. "I mean, look at the very people who are involved in this . . . the great story here for anybody willing to find it and write about it and explain it is this vast right-wing conspiracy that has been conspiring against my husband since the day he announced for President."[227]

Clinton biographer Joyce Milton describes how it was Hillary, not Bill, "who seemed to supply most of the energy. When Hillary was in residence in the White House, she would talk to Bill in the evening and get him pumped up for the next day's fight. When she was away, his attention tended to wander."[228]

On the tapes, Monica talks about filing a false affidavit and discusses her healthy fear for the Clintons' resolve.

Tripp: You—you are positive in your heart you want to do this?

Lewinsky: Uh-huh.

Tripp and Lewinsky

Tripp: I'm only saying—I'm only saying that in case you should change your mind.

Lewinsky: No. I—I—I—first of all, for fear of my life. I would not cross—I would not cross these—these people for fear of my life, number one.[229]

Nevertheless, Starr's people persauded Monica to sign an immunity agreement. She escaped jail time in exchange for handing over a blue dress stained with the President's semen. When Starr's grand jury questioned Clinton, he was forced to admit the affair.

"From the very beginning of their political career, Bill and Hillary have understood that any allegation of personal misconduct becomes a 'he said, she said' situation, in which denial is the first and best weapon to defeat scandal," wrote Dick Morris, the longtime Clinton strategist. "Until DNA testing transformed a stain on a blue dress into a trigger for impeachment, the denial defense carried them through all their scandals."[230]

Bill Clinton's wagging finger about Monica "remains the single most blatant lie ever told on national television by a President of the United States," writes Morris, "and represents an assault from which American politics has yet to recover."[231]

The lie led to impeachment hearings. Impeachment led to a trial in the Senate. But for the Clintons, the great battle only continued. Former Clinton top aide George Stephanopoulos appeared on ABC's *This Week* and said the White House was whispering about their "Ellen Rometsch" strategy.[232]

Stephanopoulos: "She was a girlfriend of John F. Kennedy, who also happened to be an East German spy. And Robert Kennedy was charged with getting her out of the country and also getting J. Edgar Hoover to go up to Congress and say, 'Don't investigate this, because if you do, we're going to open up everybody's closets.'"

Sam Donaldson: "Are you suggesting for a moment that what they're beginning to say is that if you investigate this too much, we'll put all your dirty linen right on the table? Every member of the Senate, every member of the press corp?"

Stephanopoulos: "Absolutely. The President said he would never resign, and I think some around him are willing to take everybody down with him."[233]

19.

Patrick's final hopes were placed on the top nine judges in Washington D.C. But Justice would not be obtained by Patrick through the courts. Hugh heard it first on the radio driving home in his car: the Supreme Court had refused to hear Patrick Knowlton's case.

Washington D.C. is an elite city. Political capital of the world, the lawyers and aristocrats there observe a general, unspoken rule while interacting at fancy restaurants, private clubs, and health spas: don't embarrass your Beltway colleagues.

Partisan rhetoric is fine. Healthy debate provides an appearance of rigorous scrutiny. But you should never accuse fellow attorneys, law enforcement officials, and other professionals of illegal, criminal conduct. Reserve that for the minorities, for those who live in the "fly-over zone" between D.C. and California.

Ken Starr understood this code, as do his fellow lawyers and judges in the Beltway. Miguel Rodriquez did not.

But the misdeeds of Bill Clinton were so egregious, something had to be done by Ken Starr. Linda Tripp and Monica Lewinsky provided evidence sensational enough to capture the public's nonstop attention, but the larger crimes surrounding the Clintons were not investigated.

Patrick's attorney John Clarke, by law, was permitted to see excerpts of the Final Report, without context, of the sentences that mentioned Patrick, as C2 (Citizen 2). Had he read it in its entirety, there would have been no surprises. Little was changed from Fiske's Report, except a few tweaks to better conceal embarrassing aspects of the investigation.

Knowlton attorney John Clarke

The Starr Report never mentions that the official gun was black,[234] lessening the various comments by Foster family members that Vince owned a silver gun.

Regarding the elusive x-rays, the official story started with the Park Police stating that Dr. Beyer had taken x-rays, they were readable, and they revealed no bullet fragments. Then it changed to there being no x-rays, although Beyer could not explain to the senators why Park Police believed he had taken readable x-rays. The Starr Report switches back, saying x-rays were in fact taken, despite Beyer's insistence at the hearings that they were not. Starr quotes an "unnamed assistant" who took partial, unreadable x-rays during the autopsy.[235]

Another anonymous source was used by Starr to explain the thorny, unresolved problem that Officer Rolla never found Foster's car keys. How could he drive to the park without his keys? He found his wallet, his watch, and searched all his pockets. When he visited the morgue later to search for them, they inexplicably turned up in Foster's pocket.

Had someone planted them there? Staff members at the morgue say two White House officials arrived before Rolla. Hospital manager Christina Tea described the two men as very rude and pushy, and she did not grant them permission to see the body. She insists they arrived before Rolla. Nevertheless, they prevailed. These same two men, William Kennedy and Craig Livingston, worked in the Old Executive Office Building across from the White House—possibly where Foster was headed when he was last seen by a Secret Service officer. They were both close colleagues of Hillary Clinton. They both denied arriving before Rolla, but their testimonies were suspect. They drove there together, but each testified to driving home in the other's car.[236]

Starr solved the issue by quoting an "anonymous officer" at the morgue who says the two men arrived after Rolla and only observed Foster from behind glass.[237]

**Official FBI photo of Foster's keys
(includes no Honda key)**

For his Final Report, Starr hired Dr. Henry Lee, renowned in the O.J. Simpson case, to examine evidence proving suicide. Dr. Lee's report remains secret. A clerk at the Library of Congress told Hugh it would be available in 50 years.[238]

In fact, over 75 percent of Starr's report relies on anonymous testimony and secret documents.[239]

20.

John Clarke studied the voluminous statute defining the duties of the Office of Independent Counsel and told Patrick he had a right, as a witness, to contest Starr's report in writing. If the three-judge panel, friends of Ken Starr who originally appointed him, agreed with the corrections, Patrick's contentions would be included as an Appendix to the report.

Would it make a difference, Patrick wondered. It was all now just "spitting against the wind." The three judges were Beltway men as well.

Nevertheless, Patrick and Hugh agreed with John and they drafted an eleven-page letter and nine pages of exhibits from twenty-five federal investigative records, proving six areas of cover-up. Their 20 pages were submitted to the Special Division of the U.S. Court of Appeals.

Not surprisingly, the Independent Counsel sent the judges nine pages of strenuous arguments as to why Knowlton's response—20 pages of hard-hitting documentation with evidence contradicting Starr's entire Foster ruling—should be rejected. What was surprising, however, was that Starr himself wrote the nine page argument.[240] He was no longer an uninformed, innocent bystander. He had seen the specific evidence about the gun, the neck wound, the missing head wound, the photos, the x-rays, and the massive cover-up.

The trio still had lives to lead. Patrick needed to find a way to get out of debt. Hugh was back to entertaining children and packing away the massive piles of documents scattered throughout his house.

John Clarke had a law practice to revive. He needed to find new clients while tracking down the old ones, as well as checking his mail for other opportunities. When the mail arrived on one particular business day, he did not expect to find a letter from the three-judge panel overseeing Kenneth E. Starr.

They had overruled Starr's arguments. Starr had formally petitioned the three judges to prohibit the damning appendix. But Patrick's hard-hitting evidence of Starr's corruption would be included in the final report. It was all there: the gun evidence, the neck wound, the missing exit wound, lost photos and x-rays, the keys, the cover-up, and the shady figures at the original scene.[241]

Ken Starr

There would be no appeal; this was the final ruling—despite the fact that Ken Starr had a been a colleague of all three judges on the Court of Appeals; despite the fact that the attachment contradicted the entire Foster section of Starr's report; despite the fact that this lengthy appendix would serve as history's final proclamation on what happened that day in Fort Marcy Park.

In a series of hurried faxes, Judge David Sentelle initially recommended to his two colleagues that Knowlton's motion be denied because Patrick's name was not used by Starr, only the identifer of "C2" (Civilian 2). "We could obviously deny his motion on that basis," wrote Sentelle. "The downside of that course of action is that Knowlton appears to be either a product of or a participant with the conspiracy theorists, and a denial of the motion will certainly be treated in fringe publications as an attempt to suppress his version."

But Judge Peter Fay disagreed, saying Knowlton "contradicts specific factual matters and takes issue with the very basics of the report filed by [Starr]."

"I agree that we should grant Knowlton's request," wrote the third judge, John Butzner. "I suspect that if we deny the motion we will be charged as conspirators in the cover-up."

Sentelle faxed them both back the same day and changed his position. "As we are all in agreement, it does not appear that a conference call is necessary."

The lead judge then informed the other judges he was writing Starr with a terse notice that his strenuous motion to refuse Knowlton's appendix would be denied. "I felt the less we said the better," Sentelle wrote.

As a result of the judges' decision, every library in the country would place Patrick Knowlton's detailed denunciation of Ken Starr's Final Report on their shelves, permanently.

John was shocked. Hugh was elated. Patrick felt like a POW returning home after years of isolation and torture.

The three celebrated. They prepared for the cameras and the massive onslought of the press. But it never came.

The three met with Pete Yost, lead correspondent for the *Associated Press*. They explained the magnitude of the decision. "It doesn't matter," the three say Yost told them. "It's already in the can. Suicide. Ken Starr says 'suicide,' and that's what we're reporting."[242]

Patrick, John and Hugh were stunned. Talking with him further, they realized Yost and others had indeed actually written the story of the Starr Report before it was issued.

Patrick's team had delivered the 20-page attachment to 100 media outlets, all the major ones, and Patrick himself hand-delivered the information to several key media figures, including Ted Koppel.[243]

Koppel: "I have no particular problem with where the ideology of a story comes from, as long as I can prove it to be true. Okay? You give me the evidence, I'll be delighted to broadcast it."

Miguel Rodriguez received the same treatment when he went public with his story.

Miguel: "I have talked to a number of people . . . *Time, Newsweek, Nightline, the New York Times, Boston Globe,* the Atlanta whatever, you know, there have been well over a hundred. The reporters were all genuinely interested. Reporters that I've spent a lot of time with called me back and said the editors won't allow it to go to press. The accepted media here has always had a certain take on all this. And there's been story lines from the get-go."[244]

Reed Irvine (on *Nightline*): "Miguel Rodriguez . . . prosecutor investigating this case . . . he resigned. His investigation was interfered with by his superior, a Democrat by the name of Mark Tuohey III, a close associate of the number three person in the Justice Department (Webb Hubbell). . . (Miguel) said: 'if you're not going to let me do the job as it should be done, I'm quitting. I'm going back to Sacramento.' And he did."[245]

Ted Koppel

Koppel: "I know the gentleman of whom you speak. I am familiar with the charges. The only difference with the version I have heard and the version you have recounted is that I have heard is that he is described as a guy who wanted to go off on his own, who did indeed want to follow some leads that his superiors did not want him to follow because they wanted to follow a team approach there.[246]

Miguel (on tape): "Well, I wrote that to Starr in January of this year and it was squelched by Tuohey. He could yell louder than I could. He was a team player."

21.

Who killed Vince Foster?

Many theories have emerged over the years, some so sensational as to be without merit. But three versions of the story have at least a foundation of evidence from which to develop a plausible theory.

One: Waco

Three months before his death, Vince Foster was troubled by the assault on the Branch Davidian compound in Waco, Texas, that led to 85 people killed, many of them innocent children. His assistant testified that he was working on a letter about Waco the day of this death, though this document has never surfaced.[247] If Vince Foster was about to blow the whistle on government forces that killed innocent people at Waco, powerful federal and military agencies might have reason to prevent him from doing so.

Lisa Foster told the FBI Vince "was horrified when the Branch Davidian complex burned" and believed "that everything was his fault." She mentions the problem twice, and indicated it haunted him up to his final day.[248]

Foster's secretary, Deborah Gorham, said he kept a locked filing cabinet in his office that was off limits to everyone, but she knew that he kept a file inside on the

Waco invasion. She also noted that Foster used a safe in the office of Bernie Nussbaum, Chief White House Counsel. The only time she opened it was when Foster instructed her to place in the safe two folders from the NSA (National Security Agency).[249] Other White House Counsel attorneys have said interaction is untypical between White House lawyers and the military agency that conducts worldwide clandestine surveillance and also houses the codes for a nuclear launch.

Inside the safe, Gorham said she saw two large envelopes. One had "Janet Reno," on it. The others said, "Eyes only, not to be opened, William Kennedy."[250] Kennedy, mentored by Foster, was another alumnus from the Rose Law Firm in Little Rock.

The head FBI agent at the White House, Dennis Sculimbrene, wonders why Foster was so troubled about Waco. "When you are troubled by something and feel responsible for something, you can only feel responsible for it if you could have done something about it."[251]

Foster

A member of the 1995 House Waco investigation staff believes Foster may have been in such a position.

"One of the interesting things that happens in an investigation is that you get anonymous phone calls," said investigator T. March Bell, quoted in the highly popular video *Waco: The Rules of Engagement*. "And we in fact received anonymous phone calls from Justice Department managers and attorneys who believe that pressure was placed on Janet Reno by Webb Hubbell, and pressure that came from the First Lady of the United States."[252]

At a post-screening press conference, Bell explained that phone logs suggest Hillary, Foster, and Hubbell worked on Waco together:

"Those phone logs were Webb Hubbell's phone logs. There were calls from the first lady and Vince Foster to Webb Hubbell's office" during the Waco crisis.

Bell said Hillary grew more and more impatient as the Waco standoff came to dominate the headlines during the early months of the Clinton administration. It was she, Bell's source claims, who pressured a reluctant Janet Reno to act.[253]

Years after the Waco debacle, witnesses have come forward. Former senior FBI official Danny Coulson told *Salon News* that the fires that burned the children were started by gas grenades fired into the compound, long denied by the government.[254] Also denied was any military involvement, which is unconstitutional. But former CIA officer Gene Cullen participated in meetings between the CIA and secret Delta Force military troops regarding how to handle Waco. "I was surprised at the amount of involvement they had," he told *Salon*.[255]

2. The Dixie Mafia

The *Wall Street Journal* speculated two weeks after Foster's death that he had been killed by a "military-drug cabal."[256] What was the nation's most distinguished newspaper talking about?

Bill Clinton grew up under the influence of his Uncle Raymond, a car dealer, who was quite connected to the wheelers and dealers of Hot Springs, Arkansas, where Bill was raised. In the 1960s, before Las Vegas rose to prominence, Hot Springs was named by the federal government as the largest city with illegal gambling operations in the country.[257] It was a hotbed for organized crime. When the top figures in the state later teamed up with the CIA, things really heated up.

State trooper Larry Patterson testified regarding conversations in the 1980s involving Governor Bill Clinton. The group discussed "large quantities of drugs coming into the Mena, Arkansas, airport, large quantities of money, large quantities of guns . . . [Clinton] had very little comment to make," said Patterson. "He was just listening to what was being said."[258]

The country was familiar at that time with the Iran Contra scandal, the clandestine operation run by Colonel Oliver North where weapons were flown to soldiers in Nicaragua to fight the Communists. Most Americans were, and still are, unaware of the billions worth of cocaine flown back to Arkansas on the return trips.

Russell Welch, an Arkansas official investigating the matter, wrote: "Steve Lowry (DEA) informed me in the strictest confidence that it was believed, within his department, that Barry Seal was flying weapons to central and south America in violation of U.S. foreign policy . . . In return he is allowed to smuggle what he wanted back into the United States."[259] Other reports claim Seal, after being convicted as a smuggler, appealed to the CIA to act as an informant and was embraced by then Vice-President and former CIA chief George H. W. Bush.[260]

Russell Welch
Arkansas State Police Investigator
in charge of Mena investigation

Pilot Terry Reed worked with Seal, but did not know about the drug running. When Reed, full of patriotic zeal, discovered tons of cocaine being shipped—and after Seal was assassinated by a Columbian hit squad—he left the operation. He claims his life was threatened, and he and his wife had to file suit against the Federal government to keep from being imprisoned.[261] Reed's book, *Compromised: Bush, Clinton and the CIA* has sold over 200,000 copies. Reed was dangerous due to his testimony of a private meeting he attended where Mena's activities were discussed by then Governor Bill Clinton, George Bush's future Attorney General, and "Dan Cathey," who turned out to be Oliver North.[262]

Terry Reed's wife knew Dan Cathey as well, and appreciated the dozen roses he brought her after she gave birth to a son in Little Rock.[263] She and Terry both were surprised to see him testify on national TV as Col. Oliver North.

Oliver North

Reed first met Barry Seal at Fu Lin's, the restaurant of Charlie Trie, later exposed as part of the Clinton fundraising scandal, Chinagate. At the restaurant, Seal was accompanied by Dan Lasater, a man Seal referred to as "my investment banker."[264]

In fact, Lasatar oversaw hundreds of millions in bonds.[265] He was also a friend of Bill and Roger Clinton, whom he got to know after meeting their mother, Virginia Kelly, at the Hot Springs horse racing track.[266] Lasater was ultimately convicted of social distribution of cocaine[267] in 1986, but the DEA suspected him years earlier of being a major trafficer of narcotics.

Patty-Anne Smith's testimony was used to convict Lasatar. This former girlfriend witnessed Lasater with the governor, and saw Clinton use cocaine: "He was doing a line. It was just there on the table."[268]

Patty-Anne had escaped to Florida years earlier. But it did not go as well for Charlene Wilson, a girlfriend of local prosecutor Dan Harmon. She was sentenced to 31 years[269] for a minor drug dealing charge after providing testimony of Lasator and Roger Clinton using cocaine, and also of Bill Clinton leaning against a brick wall at a bar and using coke. "He was so messed up that night," she testified. "He slid down the wall into a garbage can and just sat there like a complete idiot."[270]

Harmon's story is intertwined with the deaths of two boys on railroad tracks outside Little Rock, suspected by authorities as a spot for planes to drop crates of cocaine. Coroner Famy Malak ruled the boys were killed by the train after smoking too much marijuana and falling on the tracks.[271] But the parents insisted on another autopsy. One of the exhumed bodies revealed a large stab wound. Malak had other infamous cases, including his determination that the head of James Milam had been eaten by the family dog. However, the unbitten skull was later found. It had been decapitated with a knife.[272]

Years later, the *LA Times*, *Dateline*, and other mainstream media outlets reported Malak's favorable ruling for Clinton's mother, Virginia Kelly, a nurse anesthetist. In 1981, her 17-year-old patient was sitting up and chatting before surgery, but she never woke up. Witnesses said Kelly had fumbled the tube, but what looked like obvious malpractice was ruled "blunt trauma" by Malak, caused by a rock being thrown at the young girl's head.[273]

Charlene Wilson testified that she was in Harmon's car when he went up to get a crate of cocaine at the railroad tracks and later returned with blood all over him.[274] She believes he was involved in the murder of the two boys. A special task force was created to investigate the two boys' deaths, and, as fate would have it, Harmon was appointed to lead it. Later, Harmon put Charlene in prison for years and then harassed the DEA officer investigating his foul play.[275] Years later, Harmon was finally convicted by a jury for racketeering, extortion and drug dealing.[276] The mothers of the two boys did not see him charged for murder—and many wanted to see his larger connections with Dan Lasater exposed—but for Arkansas it was a fairly stiff conviction.

State Democratic party secretary Patsy Thomasson, a major Clinton backer, worked as Lasater's top assistant.[277] (She was later made head of drug testing in the White House.) When Roger got in trouble with the DEA, Lasater's firm had Roger drive Dan's limo for a time.[278] Later, he worked as a stable hand at a Lasater's horse farm in Ocala, Florida.[279] Roger was eventually charged and sentenced to seven years in prison for his cocaine involvement after being seriptitiously videotaped. In one famous recording, he tells an undercover office. "I've got to get some for my brother. He's got a nose like a vacuum cleaner."[280]

Roger and Bill Clinton

Roger's sentence was reduced to one year in an agreement to testify against Lasater.[281] Despite this knowledge within the Arkansas government, Lasater was awarded a $30 million bond issue for state police radios.[282] Meanwhile, a savings and loan in Chicago owned by Lasater went belly up, and the officials there sued Lasater & Company. The federal government moved in to prosecute Lasater, and the Feds hired the Rose Law firm, and specifically Hillary Clinton and Vince Foster, to lead the charge. The case ended in Lasater paying a measly $200,000 settlement. The *Chicago Sun Times* accused Hillary of a "glaring conflict of interest" since Lasater was "a family friend and an influential benefactor of her husband."[283]

Lasater's eventual conviction for social distribution of cocaine also looked like a slap on the wrist, considering that officials suspected him of heavy involvement in Barry Seal's massive cocaine operation amounting to billions of dollars in narcotics. But Lasater only served a few months of the smaller conviction. Governor Clinton pardoned him.[284]

When Trooper L.D. Brown told Clinton about large amounts of cocaine he observed at the Mena airport, Clinton immediately begged off the conversation by saying, "That's Lasater's deal."[285]

Lasater had been described by some as the kingpin of the Dixie Mafia. It wouldn't be the only place where the Clintons are associated with organized crime. Hillary's top political operative, Harold Ickes, once represented a New York union owned by the Genovese crime family that was charged with racketeering. Charles La Bella, the head of the campaign finance task force, called Ickes the "Svengali" behind every aspect of the Clinton finance scandal. The *Wall Street Journal* called Ickes "the consigliorie to the dark side of the Clinton presidency."[286]

Vince Foster spent his last days on the estate of a man associated with organized crime. Webb Hubbell spent the weekend bending Vince's ear along with Michael Cordozo, whose father-in-law, Nathan Landow, owned the plush estate on the Eastern Shore of Maryland. Landow, a renowned Democrat fundraiser, had previously been under probe by organized crime investigators for his shared casino assets with Edward Cellini, a former associate of mobster Meyer Lansky, and for shared investments with Carlo Gambino of the famed Gambino family.[287]

Webb Hubbell

It would have been hard for Webb Hubbell to literally lean on Foster that weekend, as his own elbow had been broken the day before, as reported by the *Wall Street Journal*.[288] But if indeed Foster was being heavily lobbied with "an offer he couldn't refuse," any number of sinister associations in Foster's past could have come back to haunt him.

Those dark forces included the CIA and the federal government itself, which may have given cause to Hillary Clinton's initial speculation that Foster was "assassinated by a top-secret team of navy hit men."[289] (Her initial response, according to Webb Hubbell's book.)

3. The Clinton Inner-Circle

For those who believe Foster's death was not related to larger conspiracies and cartels, a certain amount of evidence exists to show motive for the Clinton machine itself to be behind the murder.

Any number of reasons could have caused Foster to crack the week before his death and threaten to cooperate with prosecutors intent on destroying the Clinton Presidency, Watergate style. Foster was in the position of Nixon aides Mitchell, Erlichman, and Colson, and staring at years of prison time.

Travelgate was heating up. Congress had already called for an investigation, and a memo eventually surfaced showing Hillary was behind the firing of the innocent staff, along with their being harassed by the FBI and IRS.[290] Foster was still dragging his feet on placing the Clintons assets in a blind trust, which required a sworn oath regarding its accuracy. Those assets included their Whitewater property.[291] The enemies of the Clintons were smelling blood, and Hillary was battening down the hatches at every turn to prevent a meltdown.

Heavy pressure was also being placed on Foster by Hillary to regain a file on Bill's infidelities,[292] according to the wife of a private investigator in Little Rock. Jane Parks provided a lengthy interview on the subject with *London Telegraph* reporter Ambrose Evans-Pritchard. Jane was the wife of private eye Jerry Parks, who served as head of security for the 1992 Clinton-Gore campaign.[293] Jane also managed an apartment complex in the mid-80s owned by a Clinton supporter. One day she was told a resident would be needing a free apartment. It happened to be Roger Clinton, still in limbo while jobless and under investigation.[294]

Jane and her assistant, also interviewed by Ambrose, said they sometimes had to leave their offices during the day because the paper thin walls—adjoining Roger's apartment—failed to muffle the loud partying. Sometimes, the Governor would visit in his limousine, and the two brothers could be heard assessing the merits of marijuana and cocaine. "This is really good shit!" Bill told his brother.[295]

Other times, very young girls would be in the apartment. On several occasions they heard both Clintons in the middle of the day engaging in "roucous orgasms," as reported by Ambrose.[296]

Meanwhile, Jerry Parks had been hired separately by Vince Foster to spy on Bill Clinton's infidelities.[297] He made sure to photograph the comings and goings of Bill and the girls in Roger's apartment. His son Gary Parks told Ambrose about joining his father on other surveillance sessions, such as monitoring and filming the condo of Gennifer Flowers at the Quapaw Towers.[298]

Jerry Parks

Gary was watching TV with his father when the news of Vince Foster's death was reported. "I'm a dead man," he whispered.[299]

Jane says Foster would call the house on a regular basis and talk with her husband.[300] Jerry was also a friend of Barry Seal and sometimes traveled to Mena Arkansas.[301] One day Jane opened the car trunk at the grocery store to find the entire space filled with $100 bills, wrapped in string, layer after layer. "It was so full I had to sit on the trunk to get it shut again," she said.

At home she confronted her husband. "I took a handful of money and threw it in his lap and said, 'Are you running drugs?'" Jerry told her that Vince Foster paid him $1000 for each trip to Mena. He didn't know what they were up to and she said she was told to "forget what I'd seen."[302]

When Foster moved to Washington, he phoned Jerry less often. But a week before Vince died, Jane said he called Jerry to say that Hillary was upset about whether "the files" might jeopardize she and Bill. Jerry told him the files contained "plenty to hurt both of them. But you can't give her those files, that was the agreement."[303]

Jane says Vince called again, a day or two before he died, insisting he hand over the files. "You're not going to use those files," Jerry said angrily. "My name's all over that stuff. You can't give Hillary those files. Remember what she did, what you told me she did. She's capable of doing anything!"[304]

"We can trust Hil. Don't worry," said Foster.[305]

Two days later, Vince Foster was dead.

"None of the behavior following Vince Foster's suicide computed to people just mourning Vince Foster," recalled Linda Tripp, when testifying about her colleague in the White House Counsel's office. "It was far more ominous than that, and it was extremely questionable behavior on the parts of those who were immediately involved in the aftermath of his death. I felt endangered."[306]

Tripp said the atmosphere was strikingly similar when a fax came across the machine two months later announcing Jerry Parks's death. He had been gunned down by two assassins in the middle of the streets of Little Rock.

Just like with Foster, there was a "flurry of activity and the flurry of phone calls and the secrecy. I felt this was somewhat alarming," Tripp testified. "At the same time the fax was coming, phone calls were coming up to [Chief Counsel] Bernie Nussbaum, which precipitated back and forth meetings behind closed doors . . . And it created a stir, shall we say, in the Counsel's office which brought up some senior staff from the Chief of Staff's office up to the Counsel's office where they, from all appearances, went into a meeting to discuss this. It was something that they chose not to speak about."[307]

Jane Parks believes the Clintons killed her husband, as does the son Gary. A few days after his murder, someone burglarized their home and took the file he kept in his bottom dresser drawer. Gary peeked at it once, and it was filled with pictures and notations by Jerry of Bill Clinton's multitude of illicit activity.[308]

But the Jerry Parks murder was never solved. Despite sworn testimony of its importance to the White House, the murder was left unnoticed by the press. The evidence was never pursued.

If Foster's involvement with Mena's massive cocaine smuggling operation was related to his death, Ken Starr was not the right person to investigate. In fact, Starr was intimately involved with creating the legal structure to allow the CIA to more easily conduct operations like Mena and Ollie North's Iran-Contra. Starr served as key legal assistant to Attorney General William French Smith in 1982 when Smith and CIA Director William Casey finalized an agreement no longer requiring intelligence agencies to report illicit drug trafficking to lawful authorities.[309]

Smith wrote to Casey: " . . . no formal requirement regarding the reporting of narcotics has been included."

The head of the CIA responded, "I am pleased that these procedures [will] strike the proper balance between enforcement of the law and protection of intelligence sources and methods."[310]

If Foster's death involved Mena, then Starr's appointment to investigate was indeed fortuitous for drug trafficking intelligence agencies. And it would explain Starr's penchant for secrecy.

To date, Hillary Clinton has voiced no concerns over evidence of the murder of Vince Foster in the Final Report of the Office of Independent Counsel. She has made no complaint of foul play, even though her "arch enemy" Ken Starr was exposed in a cover-up by the judges who appointed him.

And Vince was her best friend.

Postscript

- Reed Irvine passed away in 2003. Patrick Knowlton and Hugh Turley were with him in the room when he died.[311]

- Brett Kavanaugh was appointed Federal Judge by George W. Bush, as was John Bates, Kavanaugh's assistant prosecutor who joined him in intimidating Patrick Knowlton.

Judge Brett Kavanaugh

- Mark Tuohey III joined a law firm defending Hillary Clinton and Vincent Foster's Rose Law Firm against the Starr investigation.[312] In 2005, Tuohey was named Washingtonian of the year.[313] In 2011, his brother-in-law Richard Daley became President Obama's Chief of Staff.

- Kenneth Starr resigned as Independent Counsel. He later advised Congress to abolish the Office of Independent Counsel, citing, among other problems, that it causes tension with the President's Justice Department, which oversees the FBI.[314]

- Miguel Rodriguez returned to Sacramento, CA, back to his/her post as Assistant U. S. Attorney. He is now "Michelle Rodriguez." He had a sex change operation.[315]

Michelle Rodriguez

- John Clarke practices law in Washington D.C. Patrick Knowlton and Hugh Turley continue to visit the National Archives every few months, hoping to find documents proving who killed Vince Foster.

- Ted Koppel continued on in the Beltway as a senior anchor for *ABC*.

  Koppel: "It is often the fringe media that will develop a story that is ultimately picked up by the mass media. If you are looking to the mass media to do the real investigative journalism, if you're looking for *Nightline* to do major investigative stories, you're looking in the wrong direction. We don't have the facilities. We don't have the time."[316]

- The shelves of major universities and libraries contain the full Starr Report, which includes Patrick Knowlton's appendix. It is technically entitled *The Report on the Death of Vincent W. Foster, Jr., by the Office of Independent Counsel In Re: Madison Guaranty Savings and Loan Association.*

- The more widely distributed version, however, of this important Presidential investigation known as the Starr Report omits Patrick's appendix and includes "The Lewinsky Affair" as a subtitle. Found in smaller libraries and sold in bookstores, this abridged version appears at the top of Google and Amazon searches for "Starr Report."[317]

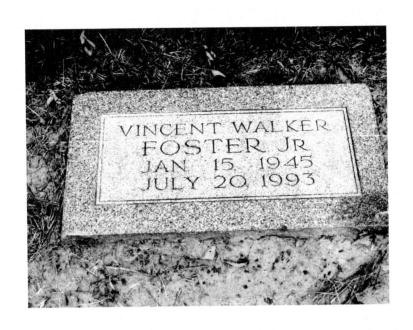

Endnotes.

Chapter 1

[1] "contruction job in Baltimore . . . registered Democrat . . ."
Author's interview with Patrick Knowlton. Quotes by Knowlton or information about his story may also be taken from author's interview with Hugh Turley and from the video interview piece "The Knowlton Project." and from John Clarke, Patrick Knowlton and Hugh Turley, *Failure of the Public Trust*, McCabe Publishing, 1999, (See also: <www.FBI-Coverup.com>)

[2] "picture taken with President Cinton . . . single mom raised him . . ."
Ibid.

[3] "get the hell out of here . . ."
John Clarke, Patrick Knowlton and Hugh Turley, *Failure of the Public Trust*, McCabe Publishing, 1999, (See also: <www.FBI-Coverup.com>), p. 294.

[4] "Maybe I'm keeping the guy . . ."
Author's interview with Patrick Knowlton.

[5] "she persuaded him it was his duty . . ."
Ibid.

[6] "threw the pictures down on his desk . . . it's brown.":
The Knowlton Project video.

[7] "smashed the headlights . . ."
The Secret Life of Bill Clinton: the unreported stories, by Ambrose Evans-Pritchard, Regnery Publishing, Washington D.C, 1997, p. 163; *Failure of the Public Trust*, p. 201.

[8] "Foster family is upset . . ."
Clarke, Knowlton and Turley, *Failure of the Public Trust*, (McCabe Publishing, 1999), p. 201, p. 267.

[9] "Gordon Liddy's radio show . . ."
Ibid.

[10] "folded over the passenger seat . . ."
Clarke, Knowlton and Turley, *Failure of the Public Trust*, (McCabe Publishing, 1999), p. 201, p. 339.

Chapter 2

[11] "hired a private detective . . ."
    Author's interview with Hugh Turley.

[12] "could not 'further identify' sinister man . . .Is this the Killer?":
    Ambrose Evans-Pritchard, *The Secret Life of Bill Clinton* (Regnery Publishing, 1997), p. 158-162.

Chapter 3

[13] "Vincenco Fosterini . . ."
    Joyce Milton, *The First Partner: Hillary Rodham Clinton*, (Perennial, 1999), p. 146.

[14] "lingerie shows . . ."
    Joyce Milton, *The First Partner: Hillary Rodham Clinton*, (Perennial, 1999), p. 92.

[15] "belly dancer . . ."
    Joyce Milton, *The First Partner: Hillary Rodham Clinton*, (Perennial, 1999), p. 146.

[16] "Hillary and Vince were sleeping with each other . . . an open secret . . ."
    Edward Klein, *The Truth about Hillary*, (Sentinal, 2005), p. 21-22.

[17] "like clockwork . . ."
    Christopher Anderson, *Bill and Hillary: The Marriage*, (William Morrow, 1999).

[18] "remote cabin out in the woods . . ."
    David Brock, "Living with the Clintons: Bill's Arkansas Bodyguards Tell the Story the Press Missed," *The American Spectator*, Jan. 1994.

[19] "Everybody knew about Hillary and Vince . . ."
    Ibid.

[20] "deep kissing, nuzzling . . ."
    Christopher Anderson, *Bill and Hillary: The Marriage*, (William

Morrow, 1999).

[21] "running tongues down each other's throats . . ."
Daniel Wattenberg, "Love and Hate in Arkansas," *The American Spectator*, May/June 1994. Cited in Joyce Milton, *The First Partner: Hillary Rodham Clinton*, (Perennial, 1999), p. 147.

[22] "I was there. I saw it."
NewsMax.com, Inside report, Oct. 30, 1998.

[23] "Look, if you're going to keep staring at me . . ."
Joyce Milton, *The First Partner: Hillary Rodham Clinton*, (Perennial, 1999), p. 48.

[24] "rough as a corn cob . . ."
Carl Bernstein, *A Woman in Charge*, (Alfred A. Knopf, '07), p.13

[25] "Head up, chin in . . ."
Edward Klein, *The Truth about Hillary*, (Sentinal, 2005), p. 50.

[26] "Don't let the doorknob . . ."
Carl Bernstein, *A Woman in Charge*, (Alfred A. Knopf, '07), p. 13.

[27] "competing 10 of 11 passes . . ."
Joyce Milton, *The First Partner: Hillary Rodham Clinton*, (Perennial, 1999), p. 13.

[28] "His ambition . . ."
Joyce Milton, *The First Partner: Hillary Rodham Clinton*, (Perennial, 1999), p. 67.

[29] "She also desired the office . . ."
Joyce Milton, *The First Partner: Hillary Rodham Clinton*, (Perennial, 1999), p. 170.

[30] "From an early age . . ."
Edward Klein, *The Truth about Hillary*, (Sentinal, 2005), p. 41.

[31] "I was less interested in Bill's political future . . ."
Joyce Milton, *The First Partner: Hillary Rodham Clinton*, (Perennial, 1999), p. 54.

[32] "If she comes to Arkansas . . ."
Joyce Milton, *The First Partner: Hillary Rodham Clinton*, (Perennial, 1999), p. 29.

[33] "she thought *she* was his fiancé . . ."

Joyce Milton, *The First Partner: Hillary Rodham Clinton*, (Perennial, 1999) p. 77.

34 "That's exactly what he did . . ."
    Edward Klein, *The Truth about Hillary*, (Sentinal, 2005), p. 84.

Chapter 4

35 " . . . Bransford delivered the subpoena . . ."
    Ambrose Evans-Pritchard, *The Secret Life of Bill Clinton* (Regnery Publishing, 1997), p. 171.

36 "But a couple of days later a strange thing happened . . . they recounted 25 different men who harassed them . . ."
    Author's interview with Patrick Knowlton; *The Knowlton Project* video.

37 "You're not going to believe what's going on here . . . to sell newspapers."
    Ambrose Evans-Pritchard, *The Secret Life of Bill Clinton* (Regnery Publishing, 1997), p. 172.

38 "call beforehand so he could have an attorney . . . get the hell out of his house . . ."
    The Knowlton Project video.

Chapter 5

39 "I'm a criminal attorney . . ."
    Author's interview with Patrick Knowlton.

40 "Patrick and John were befriended by a noted Beltway figure Reed Irvine . . . the three became a trio with a mission . . ."
    Author's interview with Hugh Turley.

41 "a known FBI tactic . . ."
    Clarke, Knowlton and Turley, *Failure of the Public Trust*, (McCabe Publishing, 1999), p. 303.

42 "Retired intelligence officers explained . . ."
    Ibid.

43 "A couple enjoying a tryst . . . or observed anything unusual."

Ambrose Evans-Pritchard, *The Secret Life of Bill Clinton* (Regnery Publishing, 1997), p. 155-158.

[44] "the license plate was white out . . ."
Ambrose Evans-Pritchard, *The Secret Life of Bill Clinton* (Regnery Publishing, 1997), p. 165.

[45] "A woman whose Mercedes had broken down . . . beat up orange compact."
Ambrose Evans-Pritchard, *The Secret Life of Bill Clinton* (Regnery Publishing, 1997), p. 166.

[46] "Did the FBI ever attempt . . . he left around 1:00 to 1:15 p.m."
Green Books, p. 50: Senate testimony of Special Agent Larry Monroe, July 29, 1994.

[47] "blonde hairs found on Foster's undershirt . . ."
Fiske Report, p. 11: Exhibit I, FBI documents.

[48] "I'm just interested to know . . . used quite often by his children."
Green Books, p. 67: Senate testimony of Special Agent Larry Monroe, July 29, 1994. See also Ambrose Evans-Pritchard, *The Secret Life of Bill Clinton* (Regnery Publishing, 1997), p. 157.

[49] "one fingerprint found on the gun."
Green Books, p. 1903. FBI Lab Memo, May 9, 1994. Cited Ambrose Evans-Pritchard, *The Secret Life of Bill Clinton* (Regnery Publishing, 1997), p. 132-133.

[50] "never run through the FBI database."
Clarke, Knowlton and Turley, *Failure of the Public Trust*, (McCabe Publishing, 1999), p. 371.

[51] ".38 caliber black revolver."
Exhibit 142, Park Police Evidence Control Receipt, by Evidence Technician Peter Simonello, July 20, 1993. Cited in Clarke, Knowlton and Turley, *Failure of the Public Trust*, (McCabe Publishing, 1999), p. 245fn.

[52] "a barrel and a butt . . . untraceable."
Green Books, p. 2056. Cited in Ambrose Evans-Pritchard, *The Secret Life of Bill Clinton* (Regnery Publishing, 1997), p. 133.

[53] "100 percent sure . . . "
Exhibit 109, Handwritten notes of FBI interview with Paramedic Richard Arthur, March 16, 1994. Cited in Clarke, Knowlton and Turley, *Failure of the Public Trust*, (McCabe Publishing, 1999),, p.

265.

[54] "nine-millimeter pistol, . . . "
　　　Exhibit 82, Report of FBI interview with Paramedic Richard Arthur, April 29, 1994. Cited in Clarke, Knowlton and Turley, *Failure of the Public Trust*, (McCabe Publishing, 1999), p. 265.

[55] "He drew a picture of both kinds of guns . . ."
　　　Exhibit 3: Arthur's drawings of revolver and automatic. Clarke, Knowlton and Turley, *Failure of the Public Trust*, (McCabe Publishing, 1999),, p. 267.

[56] "Sharon Bowman identified it . . ."
　　　Fiske Report, p. 38. Cited in Ambrose Evans-Pritchard, *The Secret Life of Bill Clinton* (Regnery Publishing, 1997),, p. 130.

[57] "Sharon thought she would be able to recognize it, . . ."
　　　Ambrose Evans-Pritchard, *The Secret Life of Bill Clinton* (Regnery Publishing, 1997), p. 131.

[58] "old piece of junk . . . He didn't remember the black handle . . ."
　　　Green Books, p. 1806. FBI 302 report, statement of Lee Foster Bowman, June 28, 1994. Cited in Ambrose Evans-Pritchard, *The Secret Life of Bill Clinton* (Regnery Publishing, 1997), p. 130.

[59] "Silver six-gun, large barrel, . . ."
　　　Green Books, p. 2153: note of Captain Hume, July 29, 1993. Cited in Evans-Pritchard, p. 130.

[60] "the gun looked similar to the one she had seen . . ."
　　　Green Books, p. 1633. FBI 302 report, interview with Lisa Foster, May 9, 1994. Cited in Ambrose Evans-Pritchard, *The Secret Life of Bill Clinton* (Regnery Publishing, 1997), p. 132.

[61] "Lisa Foster believes the gun found at Fort Marcy Park may be the silver gun . . ." Ibid.

[62] "they showed her 'a silver colored handgun' . . ."
　　　Senate Report 103-433 Vol. I, 1994. Cited in Ambrose Evans-Pritchard, *The Secret Life of Bill Clinton* (Regnery Publishing, 1997), p. 131.

Chapter 6

[63] "Bill's mom complained . . ."
> David Maraniss, *First in His Class*, (New York, Touchstone, 1995), p. 326.

[64] "I need to be fucked . . ."
> David Brock, "His Cheatin' Heart: Bill's Arkansas Bodyguards Tell the Story the Press Has Missed," *The American Spectator*, January 1994.

[65] "Betsy presented a list of 15 women to Bill, . . .Clinton knew she was right."
> David Maraniss, *First in His Class*, (New York, Touchstone, 1995)p. 440-441. See also Meredith Oakley, *On the Make: The Rise of Bill Clinton*. Regnery, 1994, p. 217. Cited in Joyce Milton, *The First Partner: Hillary Rodham Clinton*, (Perennial, 1999), p. 184.

[66] "Chelsea was too young . . . wiping a tear from her eye."
> Dick Morris, *Rewriting History*, (HarperCollins, 2004), p. 197.

[67] "Vince Foster kept the list for Hillary, . . ."
> Joyce Milton, *The First Partner: Hillary Rodham Clinton*, (Perennial, 1999), p. 212-213.

Chapter 7

[68] "They examined documents late into the night, . . . if he chose to go that route."
> Author's interviews with Patrick Knowlton and Hugh Turley.

[69] "There is no other trauma identified . . . It is exceedingly unlikely . . ."
> Ambrose Evans-Pritchard, *The Secret Life of Bill Clinton* (Regnery Publishing, 1997), p. 142-143.

[70] "of the 26 people at the death scene, . . ."
> Clarke, Knowlton and Turley, *Failure of the Public Trust*, (McCabe Publishing, 1999), p. 152.

[71] "might expect if an assassin was pressing a gun . . ."
> Ambrose Evans-Pritchard, *The Secret Life of Bill Clinton* (Regnery Publishing, 1997), p. 140-141.

[72] "trauma to the neck"
> Exhibit 103, Medical Examiner Report of Investigation by Dr.

Donald Haut, July 20, 1993. Clarke, Knowlton and Turley, *Failure of the Public Trust*, (McCabe Publishing, 1999*)*, p. 202.

[73] "low velocity weapon."

Exhibit 73, Report of FBI interview of Dr. Donald Haut, April 12, 1994. Cited in Clarke, Knowlton and Turley, *Failure of the Public Trust*, (McCabe Publishing, 1999*)*, p. 174.

[74] "a small gunshot wound here near the jawline, . . ."

Green Books, p. 892, deposition of Richard Arthur, July 14, 1994. Cited in Ambrose Evans-Pritchard, *The Secret Life of Bill Clinton* (Regnery Publishing, 1997), p. 143.

[75] "Lt. Bianchi told me from orders higher up . . ."

Ibid.

[76] "mushy spot . . ."

Exhibit 6, Deposition of Park Police Investigator John Rolla, July 21, 1994. Cited in Clarke, Knowlton and Turley, *Failure of the Public Trust*, (McCabe Publishing, 1999*),*, p. 170-171.

[77] "I still can't believe that the hole . . ."

Ibid.

Chapter 8

[78] "Patrick continued to talk with John and Turley . . . handed the clerk a lawsuit."

Author's interview with Patrick Knowlton.

[79] "Freedom of Information Act lawsuit . . ."

Ambrose Evans-Pritchard, *The Secret Life of Bill Clinton* (Regnery Publishing, 1997), p. 146.

[80] "The lady in the Mercedes . . . mention an orange car, but the 302 does not."

Ambrose Evans-Pritchard, *The Secret Life of Bill Clinton* (Regnery Publishing, 1997), p. 166.

[81] "purpose for lifting the body . . ."

Exhibit 121, Report of FBI interview Dr. Julian Orenstein, April 14, 1994. Cited in Clarke, Knowlton and Turley, *Failure of the Public Trust*, (McCabe Publishing, 1999*)*, p. 177.

[82] "The handwritten notes say nothing about an exit wound . . ."
FBI notes, p. 287, notes on interview with Orenstein. Cited in
Ambrose Evans-Pritchard, *The Secret Life of Bill Clinton* (Regnery
Publishing, 1997), p. 146.

[83] "I never saw one directly, . . ."
Ambrose Evans-Pritchard, *The Secret Life of Bill Clinton* (Regnery
Publishing, 1997), p. 145.

[84] "The photographs taken . . ."
Ambrose Evans-Pritchard, *The Secret Life of Bill Clinton* (Regnery
Publishing, 1997), p. 144.

[85] "Back of head . . . Redacted."
FBI notes, p. 196.

[86] "license plate . . ."
Green Books, p. 2390: Park Police photographs. Cited in Ambrose
Evans-Pritchard, *The Secret Life of Bill Clinton* (Regnery
Publishing, 1997), p. 165.

[87] "As was Lisa Foster's 302 . . ."
FBI 302 report, statement of Lisa Foster, May 9, 1994. Ambrose
Evans-Pritchard, *The Secret Life of Bill Clinton* (Regnery
Publishing, 1997), p. 146.

Chapter 9

[88] "obscene . . ."
Senate Banking Committee Hearings, July 29, 1994.

[89] "Let's assume for the sake of argument . . ."
"Death of Vince Foster-Part 4," Accuracy in Media tape
transcription, Oct. 16, 2004.

[90] "x-rays indicated there was no evidence of bullet fragments . . ."
Supplemental Criminal Incident Record of the U.S. Park Police,
Green Books, p. 2128. Cited in Ambrose Evans-Pritchard, *The
Secret Life of Bill Clinton* (Regnery Publishing, 1997), p. 146.

[91] "Dr. Beyer, your autopsy report . . . I have no explanation."
Exhibit 125, Testimony of Dr. James C. Beyer before the United
States Senate Banking Committee, July 29, 1994. Cited in Clarke,
Knowlton and Turley, Failure of the Public Trust, (McCabe

Publishing, 1999), p. 192.

[92] "the example of Tommy Burkett . . ."
Christopher Ruddy, *The Strange Death of Vincent Foster: An Investigation*, (The Free Press, 1997), p. 275-277.

[93] "Beyer is nothing but a stooge . . ."
Ambrose Evans-Pritchard, *The Secret Life of Bill Clinton* (Regnery Publishing, 1997), p. 149.

[94] "The case of Timothy Easley . . . girlfriend confessed . . ."
Christopher Ruddy, *The Strange Death of Vincent Foster,* (The Free Press, 1997), p. 275-277.

[95] "Fine, whether the coroner's report says that . . ."
Green Books, p. 892, deposition of Richard Arthur, July 14, 1994. Cited in Ambrose Evans-Pritchard, *The Secret Life of Bill Clinton* (Regnery Publishing, 1997), p. 143.

Chapter 10

[96] "Mallory, . . ."
Joyce Milton, *The First Partner: Hillary Rodham Clinton*, (Perennial, 1999), p. 69-70.

[97] "someone warned her to keep her mouth shut . . ."
Joyce Milton, *The First Partner: Hillary Rodham Clinton*, (Perennial, 1999), p. 225, 235.

[98] "Elizabeth Ward Gracen . . . She agreed to make a statement . . ."
Richard Johnson, "How Liz Gracen Got Her Big Break," New York Post Online. Cited in Joyce Milton, *The First Partner: Hillary Rodham Clinton*, (Perennial, 1999), p. 226-227.

[99] "Former Miss Arkansas Sally Perdue . . . it never aired."
Joyce Milton, *The First Partner: Hillary Rodham Clinton*, (Perennial, 1999), p. 233.

[100] "Flowers met Clinton . . . Bill's morning runs."\
Joyce Milton, *The First Partner: Hillary Rodham Clinton*, (Perennial, 1999), p. 94, 169.

[101] "Flowers was hired to sing . . . 'No, you go ahead.'"
Joyce Milton, *The First Partner: Hillary Rodham Clinton*,

(Perennial, 1999), p. 169.

[102] "abortion"
>   Joyce Milton, *The First Partner: Hillary Rodham Clinton*, (Perennial, 1999), p. 94.

[103] "Gennifer soon had a state job . . ."
>   Joyce Milton, *The First Partner: Hillary Rodham Clinton*, (Perennial, 1999), p. 207-208.

[104] "If they ever hit you with it . . . no problem."
>   Sam Smith, "Arkansas Connections: A time line of the rise and fall of Clinton and friends," (Year 1992 of Timeline), *Progressive Review*, 1998.

[105] "As Flower's hearing neared, . . . 'better off dead' . . ."
>   Joyce Milton, *The First Partner: Hillary Rodham Clinton*, (Perennial, 1999), p. 218-219.

[106] "Jack Palladino had been hired . . ."
>   Dick Morris, *Rewriting History*, (HarperCollins, 2004), p. 201-202.

[107] "Is Gennifer the kind of person . . ."
>   Joyce Milton, *The First Partner: Hillary Rodham Clinton*, (Perennial, 1999), p. 232.

[108] "Dolly Kyle Browning later admitted . . ."
>   Joyce Milton, *The First Partner: Hillary Rodham Clinton*, (Perennial, 1999), p. 225, 235.

[109] "pretty little legs . . ."
>   Joyce Milton, *The First Partner: Hillary Rodham Clinton*, (Perennial, 1999), p. 233.

[110] "You eat good pussy . . . coaching to deny everything."
>   Joyce Milton, *The First Partner: Hillary Rodham Clinton*, (Perennial, 1999), p. 208.

[111] "Anthony Pellicano . . . grenades and other explosives."
>   Dick Morris, *Rewriting History*, (HarperCollins, 2004), p. 202-203.

[112] "That allegation is false . . . zone of privacy for everyone."
>   Joyce Milton, *The First Partner: Hillary Rodham Clinton*, (Perennial, 1999), p. 220-221.

[113] "Tammy Wynette . . ."
    Joyce Milton, *The First Partner: Hillary Rodham Clinton*, (Perennial, 1999), p. 221.

[114] "on record denying it . . ."
    Sam Smith, "Arkansas Connections," Year 1992 of Timeline.

Chapter 11

[115] "a retired police captain . . . just a dispute over a parking space."
    Ambrose Evans-Pritchard, *The Secret Life of Bill Clinton* (Regnery Publishing, 1997), p. 163-164.

[116] "worked for the FBI, as well as 'Active SCI,' . . . "
    Ibid. The security credential document is reprinted on p. 416.

[117] "foreboding news began to leak . . . it was intended as sabotage."
    Ambrose Evans-Pritchard, *The Secret Life of Bill Clinton* (Regnery Publishing, 1997), p. 111-112.

Chapter 12

[118] "Miguel Rodriguez . . . diverse and tolerant."
    Ambrose Evans-Pritchard, *The Secret Life of Bill Clinton* (Regnery Publishing, 1997), p. 111-112.

[119] "Fiske himself indicated . . ."
    "Death of Vince Foster: Parts 1- 4," Accuracy in Media tape transcription of phone calls with Miguel Rodriguez, Oct. 16, 2004. The phone calls themselves are also available on CD.

[120] "Mark Tuohey III, did not see it that way . . ."
    Ambrose Evans-Pritchard, *The Secret Life of Bill Clinton* (Regnery Publishing, 1997), p. 138.

[121] "Illinois has long legacy of public corruption: at least 79 elected officials have been convicted of wrongdoing since 1972." Staff and news service reports, Dec. 9, 2008.

[122] "There is no evidence that that gun . . ."
    "Death of Vince Foster: Parts 1- 4." Accuracy in Media phone recordings of Miguel Rodriquez.

[123] "Even the Park Police . . ."
Ibid.

[124] "he saw men running away . . ."
FBI 302 report of Todd Hall, March 18, 1994. Cited in Evans-Pritchard, p. 125.

[125] "it could have possibly been cars . . ."
FBI 302 report of Todd Hall, April 27, 1994. Cited in Evans-Pritchard, p. 125.

[126] "Both EMTs that responded . . ."
"Death of Vince Foster: Parts 1- 4." Accuracy in Media phone recordings of Miguel Rodriquez.

[127] "but what he saw was people . . ."
Interview with confidential grand jury source. Ambrose Evans-Pritchard, *The Secret Life of Bill Clinton* (Regnery Publishing, 1997), p. 125.

[128] "I saw pictures that clearly indicate . . ."
"Death of Vince Foster: Parts 1- 4." Accuracy in Media phone recordings of Miguel Rodriquez.

[129] "this is a quote: 'Back off . . .'"
Ibid.

[130] "What does this guy Knowlton have to gain . . . the guy is a damn hero."
Ibid.

Chapter 13

[131] "Hillary insisted on an office in the West Wing . . ."
Edward Klein, *The Truth about Hillary*, (Sentinal, 2005), p. 106.

[132] "Hillary for President."
Edward Klein, *The Truth about Hillary*, (Sentinal, 2005), p. 42.

[133] "the strange characters . . ."
Edward Klein, *The Truth about Hillary*, (Sentinal, 2005), p. 107.

[134] "Christmastime brought new ideas for decoration . . ."
Sam Smith, "Arkansas Connections," Year 1994 of Timeline.

[135] "syringes and roach clips . . ."
        Ibid.

[136] "had not passed their drug tests . . . Hillary chose personal confidente Patsy Thomasson . . ."
        Joyce Milton, *The First Partner: Hillary Rodham Clinton*, (Perennial, 1999), p. 273.

[137] "While Lasatar was in jail, Patsy ran the company . . ."
        Sam Smith, "Arkansas Connections," Year 1996 of Timeline.

[138] "a memo listing the dozen or so scandals . . ."
        Joyce Milton, *The First Partner: Hillary Rodham Clinton*, (Perennial, 1999), p. 321.

[139] "Fix it, Vince!"
        Joyce Milton, *The First Partner: Hillary Rodham Clinton*, (Perennial, 1999), p. 287.

[140] "Bob Dole called for an investigation . . ."
        Christopher Ruddy, *The Strange Death of Vincent Foster,* (The Free Press, 1997), p. 262.

[141] "a subpoena was issued . . ."
        Ibid.

[142] "Vince and his wife Lisa headed to a remote hotel . . . was relaxed and leisurely . . ."
        FBI 302 of Webster Hubbell, April 13, 1994; FBI 302 of Lisa Foster, April 12, 1994. Cited in Ambrose Evans-Pritchard, *The Secret Life of Bill Clinton* (Regnery Publishing, 1997), p. 223.

[143] "It had not gone particularly well."
        FBI 302 of Lisa Foster, May 9, 1994. Cited in Ambrose Evans-Pritchard, *The Secret Life of Bill Clinton* (Regnery Publishing, 1997), p. 223.

[144] Webb Hubbell stopped in twice . . . for a closed door meeting . . ."
        FBI 302 of Deborah Gorham, June 23, 1994; FBI 302 of Marsha Scott, June 9, 1994. Cited in Evans-Pritchard, p. 224.

[145] "It lasted two hours . . ."
        FBI 302 of Linda Tripp, April 12, 1994. Cited in Ambrose Evans-Pritchard, *The Secret Life of Bill Clinton* (Regnery Publishing, 1997), p. 224.

[146] "If I see Bill before you do . . ."
>
> FBI notes of Marsha Scott, p. 353. Cited in Ambrose Evans-Pritchard, *The Secret Life of Bill Clinton* (Regnery Publishing, 1997), p. 224.

[147] "Clinton called Foster at his home . . . Clint Eastwood's 'In the Line of Fire' . . ."
>
> Green Books, p. 1829: deposition of President Clinton June 12, 1994. Cited in Ambrose Evans-Pritchard, *The Secret Life of Bill Clinton* (Regnery Publishing, 1997), p. 225.

[148] "He drove his kids to their workplaces . . ."
>
> Ambrose Evans-Pritchard, *The Secret Life of Bill Clinton* (Regnery Publishing, 1997), p. 227.

[149] "working on a memo about the Waco disaster . . ."
>
> SWSC deposition of Tom Castleton, June 27, 1995: comment by majority counsel Michael Chertoff. Cited in Ambrose Evans-Pritchard, *The Secret Life of Bill Clinton* (Regnery Publishing, 1997), p. 221.

[150] "some M&Ms, said he would be back . . ."
>
> Exhibit 38, Report of FBI interview of Executive Assistant Linda Tripp, April 12, 1994. Cited in Clarke, Knowlton and Turley, *Failure of the Public Trust*, (McCabe Publishing, 1999), p. 49.

[151] "last seen by the downstairs Secret Service agent . . ."
>
> Exhibit 49, Report of FBI interview of US Secret Service Officer John S. Skyles, April 21, 1994. Cited in Clarke, Knowlton and Turley, *Failure of the Public Trust*, (McCabe Publishing, 1999), p. 55, 382.

[152] "Hillary says . . . 'the last specific conversation I can recall . . . And that's it.'"
>
> Robert Fiske deposition of Hillary Clinton, June 12, 1994. Cited in Hugh Turley and Mark Wright, "Former White House Aide Contradicts Hillary," Unpublished article, Sept. 2007.

[153] "Hillary Clinton in Vincent Foster's office approximately four times . . ."
>
> FBI 302 report of Thomas Castleton, May 3, 1994. Cited in Hugh Turley and Mark Wright, "Former White House Aide Contradicts Hillary," Unpublished article, Sept. 2007.

[154] "Patrick and Hugh Turley found it . . ."
>
> Author's interview with Hugh Turley.

[155] "pretty pumped up about the whole thing . . . I spent the night in his bed'"

Rebecca Borders, "Hell to Pay," *The American Spectator*, Jan. 1997. Cited in Ambrose Evans-Pritchard, *The Secret Life of Bill Clinton* (Regnery Publishing, 1997), p. 224.

Chapter 14

[156] "Kavanaugh: "The question is whether there is evidence . . .screwed up on colors . . ."
"Death of Vince Foster: Part 3." Accuracy in Media phone recordings of Brett Kavanaugh.

[157] "It's not just Tuohey . . ."
"Death of Vince Foster: Parts 1- 4," Accuracy in Media tape transcription of phone calls with Miguel Rodriguez.

[158] "felt compelled to read the perjury statute . . ."
Ambrose Evans-Pritchard, *The Secret Life of Bill Clinton* (Regnery Publishing, 1997), p. 149.

[159] "seven polaroids were snatched up . . ."
Exhibit 96, Report of FBI interview of Park Police Officer Franz Ferstl, May 2, 1994. Cited in Clarke, Knowlton and Turley, *Failure of the Public Trust*, (McCabe Publishing, 1999), p. 132.

[160] "I mean, I had them in the office that night . . ."
Green Books, p. 652: Senate deposition of Detective John Rolla, July 21, 1994. Cited in Ambrose Evans-Pritchard, *The Secret Life of Bill Clinton* (Regnery Publishing, 1997), p. 375.

[161] "His camera has never failed before or since . . ."
Exhibit 104, Deposition of Park Police Identification Technician Peter Simonello, July 14, 1994. Cited in Clarke, Knowlton and Turley, *Failure of the Public Trust*, (McCabe Publishing, 1999), p. 147.

[162] "pretty clear . . ."
Exhibit 107, Deposition of Paramedic Richard Arthur, July 14, 1994. Cited in Clarke, Knowlton and Turley, *Failure of the Public Trust*, (McCabe Publishing, 1999), p. 151.

[163] "looked good to me . . ."
Exhibit 104, Deposition of Park Police Identification Technician Peter Simonello, July 14, 1994. Cited in Clarke, Knowlton and Turley, *Failure of the Public Trust*, (McCabe Publishing, 1999), p.

150.

[164] "the photographs that were taken for several people don't exist any longer . . ."

"Death of Vince Foster: Parts 1- 4," Accuracy in Media tape transcription of phone calls with Miguel Rodriguez.

[165] "original 911 call no longer exists . . . second . . . sounds staged . . ."
Author's interview with Hugh Turley.

[166] "a private citizen found Foster with no gun . . ."
For the story of this "Confidential Witness," see Ambrose Evans-Pritchard, *The Secret Life of Bill Clinton* (Regnery Publishing, 1997), p. 120-123.

[167] "Officer Kevin Fornshill . . . guard the entrace to the CIA . . ."
Green Books: deposition of Kevin Fornshill, July 12, 1994. Cited in Ambrose Evans-Pritchard, *The Secret Life of Bill Clinton* (Regnery Publishing, 1997),. 124.

[168] "Fornshill was not interviewed for a year . . ."
Clarke, Knowlton and Turley, *Failure of the Public Trust*, (McCabe Publishing, 1999), p. 164.

[169] "Did any of the detectives . . . No, not that I know of."
Exhibit 79, Deposition of Park Police Officer Kevin Fornshill, July 12, 1994. Cited in Clarke, Knowlton and Turley, *Failure of the Public Trust*, (McCabe Publishing, 1999), p. 164.

[170] "He suggested the two of them search for the body up to the left . . . find the Foster body immediately."
Ibid.

[171] "he saw men running away . . ."
FBI 302 report of Todd Hall, March 18, 1994. Cited in Ambrose Evans-Pritchard, *The Secret Life of Bill Clinton* (Regnery Publishing, 1997), p. 125.

[172] "Gonzales then arrived . . ."
Clarke, Knowlton and Turley, *Failure of the Public Trust*, (McCabe Publishing, 1999), p. 78-114. Clarke, Knowlton, and Turley provide a highly detailed, step-by-step, documented account of every movement of personnel at the crime scene that evening, complete with charts and citations.

[173] "I didn't know who this guy was . . ."
Exhibit 6, Deposition of Park Police Investigator John Rolla, July 21,

1994. Cited in Clarke, Knowlton and Turley, *Failure of the Public Trust*, (McCabe Publishing, 1999), p. 135.

[174] "Edwards gave directions . . . ordered him to return to the parking lot."
See Clarke, Knowlton and Turley, *Failure of the Public Trust*, (McCabe Publishing, 1999), p. 90-91.

[175] "now holding a .38 caliber revolver . . ."
Exhibit 113, Park Police Incident Report, by Park Police Investigator John Rolla, July 21, 1993. "Investigator John Rolla, the thirteenth person to see the body, was the first to report that he 'observed a dark colored revolver in Mr. Foster's right hand.'" Clarke, Knowlton and Turley, *Failure of the Public Trust*, (McCabe Publishing, 1999), p. 271.

[176] "Miguel believed it had likely been planted . . ."
Ambrose Evans-Pritchard, *The Secret Life of Bill Clinton* (Regnery Publishing, 1997), p. 112. Miguel Rodriguez Memo, Dec. 9, 1994, "Meeting of Nov. 29, 1994 Concerning Foster Death Matter and Supplemental Investigation Prior to Grand Jury." p. 22

[177] "accounts of a blood spill . . ."
Clarke, Knowlton and Turley, *Failure of the Public Trust*, (McCabe Publishing, 1999), p. 102.

[178] "fresh blood which several did not see . . ."
Fornshill testified that the blood was "dried... dark in color... [and] flaking." Gonzalez testified that the blood he saw was "dry." Hall saw blood on the collar but not on face or shirt, and said that the photos showed blood that he did not see. Arthur testified the blood was not running. Pisani saw no blood on the face and said that the photographs showed more blood than he saw. Ferstl saw a small amount of blood around the mouth, which was "not fresh." Clarke, Knowlton and Turley, *Failure of the Public Trust*, (McCabe Publishing, 1999), p. 152-153.

[179] "The one and only interview . . . remains secret."
Clarke, Knowlton and Turley, *Failure of the Public Trust*, (McCabe Publishing, 1999), p. 132..

[180] "God! I'm just brimming over . . ."
"Death of Vince Foster: Parts 1- 4," Accuracy in Media tape transcription of phone calls with Miguel Rodriguez.

Chapter 15

[181] National Archives document, 102-525 (JFK ACI) released March 15, 2007. See fbicover-up.com/vince-foster-document.html

[182] "Even suppose some covered things up . . ."
"Death of Vince Foster: Part 4," Accuracy in Media tape transcription of Ted Koppel's conversation with Reed Irvine on ABC's *Nightline*.

[183] "Everyone makes a very big mistake . . ."
"Death of Vince Foster: Parts 1- 4," Accuracy in Media tape transcription of phone calls with Miguel Rodriguez.

[184] "The same agency . . ."
See Ambrose Evans-Pritchard, *The Secret Life of Bill Clinton* (Regnery Publishing, 1997), p. 139-140.

[185] "I said, 'Look, I think it might be a good idea to use different FBI agents . . .'"
"Death of Vince Foster: Parts 1- 4," Accuracy in Media tape transcription of phone calls with Miguel Rodriguez.

[186] "A famous photograph released by ABC . . ."
Christopher Ruddy, *The Strange Death of Vincent Foster,* (The Free Press, 1997), Pictures insert.

[187] " . . . other items with limited value."
Ambrose Evans-Pritchard, *The Secret Life of Bill Clinton* (Regnery Publishing, 1997), p. 142.

[188] "Thanks to an insider . . .deliberately withheld . . ."
Ambrose Evans-Pritchard, *The Secret Life of Bill Clinton* (Regnery Publishing, 1997), p. 140.

[189] "I had to go through great lengths to get it . . ."
"Death of Vince Foster: Parts 1- 4," Accuracy in Media tape transcription of phone calls with Miguel Rodriguez.

[190] "The neck wound had been smeared . . ."
Evans-Pritchard, p. 140.

[191] "That was a Polaroid, a picture of a picture of a picture . . ."
"Death of Vince Foster: Parts 1- 4," Accuracy in Media tape transcription of phone calls with Miguel Rodriguez.

[192] "It is my unequivocal, categorical opinion . . ."
Senate testimony of Charles Hirsch, July 29, 1994.

[193] "One Park Police Officer had already confessed . . ."
Ambrose Evans-Pritchard, *The Secret Life of Bill Clinton* (Regnery Publishing, 1997), p. 149.

[194] "I was unable to call witnesses . . ."
"Death of Vince Foster: Parts 1- 4," Accuracy in Media tape transcription of phone calls with Miguel Rodriguez.

[195] Hickman Ewing memo of Feb. 10, 1995 meeting with Miguel Rodriguez. National Archives 102-526 (JFK ACT), released Dec. 16, 2009. See http://www.dcdave.com/article5/EwingTuoheyRambusch.pdf

Chapter 16

[196] "Christy Zircher . . . the *Post*, which never wrote the story."
Joyce Milton, *The First Partner: Hillary Rodham Clinton*, (Perennial, 1999), p. 241-242.

[197] "Kiss it."
Paula Jones vs. William Jefferson Clinton, filed May 6, 1994.

[198] "Hillary refused. Bennett was surprised . . ."
Edward Klein, *The Truth about Hillary*, (Sentinal, 2005), p. 30.

[199] "headed to a resort in the Carribbean . . . admitted to a single sexual encounter . . ."
Joyce Milton, *The First Partner: Hillary Rodham Clinton*, (Perennial, 1999), p. 226-227.

[200] "Clinton groped her. Once again, Linda Tripp was a witness. . ."
Joyce Milton, *The First Partner: Hillary Rodham Clinton*, (Perennial, 1999), p. 393-394.

[201] "asked if she got the message."
Dick Morris, *Rewriting History*, (HarperCollins, 2004), p.

[202] "Terry W. Good admitted . . ."
Joyce Milton, *The First Partner: Hillary Rodham Clinton*, (Perennial, 1999), p. 398.

[203] "Lenzner claimed privilege . . . Brooke Shearer . . . Raymond Kelly . . ."
Joyce Milton, *The First Partner: Hillary Rodham Clinton*, (Perennial, 1999), p. 244.

[204] "you motherfucker . . ."
Joyce Milton, *The First Partner: Hillary Rodham Clinton*, (Perennial, 1999), p. 262.

[205] "White House secret police."
Dick Morris, *Rewriting History*, (HarperCollins, 2004), p. 206.

[206] "The use of detectives to scour the backgrounds . . ."
Dick Morris, *Rewriting History*, (HarperCollins, 2004), p. 200.

[207] "she willingly signed an affidavit . . ."
Joyce Milton, *The First Partner: Hillary Rodham Clinton*, (Perennial, 1999), p. 395.

[208] "He thought he could take care of the questions . . . smug, cocky, arrogant."
Edward Klein, *The Truth about Hillary*, (Sentinal, 2005), p. 34-35.

[209] Ibid.

[210] "This is not going to be proven true . . ."
Dick Morris, *Rewriting History*, (HarperCollins, 2004), p. 215.

Chapter 17

[211] "Patrick sat at a table by himself . . ."
This account taken primarily from Clarke, Knowlton and Turley, *Failure of the Public Trust*, (McCabe Publishing, 1999), p. 326-333.

[212] "Did he touch your genitals?"
Ambrose Evans-Pritchard, *The Secret Life of Bill Clinton* (Regnery Publishing, 1997), p. 174.

[213] "Who asked him if he touched his genitals? . . . I can't believe Brett did that."
"Death of Vince Foster: Parts 1- 4," Accuracy in Media tape transcription of phone calls with Miguel Rodriguez.

[214] "Patrick was in debt . . ."
Author's interviews with Patrick Knowlton and Hugh Turley.

[215] "he and Turley would head to the National Archives . . ."
Ibid.

[216] "what was clearly whited-out . . . type instead was the word 'head.'"
Haut Report, July 20, 1993. Office of Chief Medical Examiner.
Cited in Evans-Pritchard, p. 142-143.

[217] "Gunshot, mouth to neck."
Ibid.

[218] "The Independent Counsel themselves, and the FBI, beat me back . . ."
"Death of Vince Foster: Parts 1- 4," Accuracy in Media tape
transcription of phone calls with Miguel Rodriguez.

[219] "I have been communicated with again . . ."
Ibid.

[220] "Starr took it under advisement but did nothing . . ."
Christopher Ruddy, "Policy Dispute Led to Foster Probe
Shakeup," *NewsMax .com*, May 3, 1995. See also Evans-Pritchard,
p. 151.

[221] Miguel Rodriguez Memo, Dec. 9, 1994, "Meeting of Nov. 29, 1994
Concerning Foster Death Matter and Supplemental Investigation Prior to
Grand Jury." National Archives document, 102-506 (JFK Act), released
Nov. 27, 2009.

[222] Miguel Rodrigues letter to Kenneth W. Starr, Jan. 17, 1995. National
Archives, 102-506 (JFK Act), released Dec. 16, 2009. See
http://www.fbicover-
up.com/ewExternalFiles/Miquel%20resignation%20ltr.pdf

[223] "I knew what the result was going to be . . ."
"Death of Vince Foster: Parts 1- 4," Accuracy in Media tape
transcription of phone calls with Miguel Rodriguez.

[224] "The result is being dictated . . ."
Ibid.

Chapter 18

[225] "Sid Blumenthal was spreading rumors . . ."
Edward Klein, *The Truth about Hillary*, (Sentinal, 2005), p. 127.

[226] "Jim Leach . . . burglar rifled through the car of Cheryl Mills . . ."
Sam Smith, "Arkansas Connections: A time line of the rise and fall of Clinton and friends," (Year 1994 of Timeline), *Progressive Review*, 1998.

[227] "I do believe this is a battle . . ."
Joyce Milton, *The First Partner: Hillary Rodham Clinton*, (Perennial, 1999), p. 7.

[228] "it was Hillary, not Bill, 'who seemed to supply most of the energy . . .'"
Joyce Milton, *The First Partner: Hillary Rodham Clinton*, (Perennial, 1999), p. 398.

[229] "I would not cross these—these people for fear of my life . . ."
Sam Smith, "Arkansas Connections: A time line of the rise and fall of Clinton and friends," (Year 1998 of Timeline), *Progressive Review*, 1998.

[230] "Until DNA testing transformed a stain on a blue dress . . ."
Dick Morris, *Rewriting History*, (HarperCollins, 2004), p. 208.

[231] "remains the single most blatant lie . . ."
Dick Morris, *Rewriting History*, (HarperCollins, 2004), p. 15.

[232] "Stephanopoulos . . . 'Ellen Rometsch' strategy . . ."
Sam Smith, "Arkansas Connections: A time line of the rise and fall of Clinton and friends," (Year 1998 of Timeline), *Progressive Review*, 1998.

[233] "Are you suggesting . . .? Absolutely . . ."
Ibid.

Chapter 19

[234] "never mentions that the official gun was black . . ."
Clarke, Knowlton and Turley, *Failure of the Public Trust*, (McCabe Publishing, 1999), p. 277.

[235] "The Starr Report switches back . . . unnamed assistant . . ."
Clarke, Knowlton and Turley, *Failure of the Public Trust*, (McCabe Publishing, 1999), p. 189-190.

[236] "Officer Rolla never found Foster's car keys . . . Christina Tea . . .

William Kennedy and Craig Livingston . . ."
    Clarke, Knowlton and Turley, *Failure of the Public Trust,*
(McCabe Publishing, 1999), p. 339-358. See also Evans-Pritchard, p. 167-170.

[237] "'anonymous officer' at the morgue . . ."
    Clarke, Knowlton and Turley, *Failure of the Public Trust,*
(McCabe Publishing, 1999), p. 353.

[238] "Dr. Lee's report remains secret . . . 50 years."
    Clarke, Knowlton and Turley, *Failure of the Public Trust,*
(McCabe Publishing, 1999), p. 389.

[239] "75 percent of Starr's report . . ."
    Clarke, Knowlton and Turley, *Failure of the Public Trust,*
(McCabe Publishing, 1999), p. 116.

Chapter 20

[240] "Starr himself wrote the nine page argument . . ."
    Author's interview with Patrick Knowlton and Hugh Turley. Most
OIC documents were not signed by Starr, including the OIC's report on
Foster's death. This nine page argument was signed by Starr. See Starr's
motion: http://www.fbicover-up.com/ewExternalFiles/Butznerpapers.pdf

[241] For the actual 20-page attachment, see <FBICover-Up.com>.

[242] "It's already in the can. Suicide."
    Author's interview with Patrick Knowlton and Hugh Turley.

[243] "delivered the 20-page attachment to 100 media outlets . . . including Ted
Koppel."
    Ibid.

[244] "I have talked to a number of people . . . Time, Newsweek, Nightline . . ."
    "Death of Vince Foster: Parts 1- 4," Accuracy in Media tape
    transcription of phone calls with Miguel Rodriguez.

[245] "Miguel Rodriguez, the top Foster prosecutor for Ken Starr, resigned in
disgust . . ."
    "Death of Vince Foster: Parts 4," Accuracy in Media tape
    transcription of ABC's *Nightline*: Interview of Reed Irvine by Ted
    Koppel.

[246] "I know the gentleman . . . they wanted to follow a team approach . . ."
"Death of Vince Foster: Parts 4," Accuracy in Media tape
transcription of ABC's *Nightline*: Interview of Reed Irvine by Ted
Koppel.

Chapter 21

[247] "working on a letter about Waco . . ."
Senate Whitewater Special Committee: Deposition of Tom
Castleton, June 27, 1995: comment by majority counsel Michael
Chertoff. Cited in Ambrose Evans-Pritchard, *The Secret Life of
Bill Clinton* (Regnery Publishing, 1997), p. 221.

[248] "Lisa Foster told the FBI Vince 'was horrified . . ."
FBI 302 report, statement of Lisa Foster, April 12, 1994. Cited in
Ambrose Evans-Pritchard, *The Secret Life of Bill Clinton* (Regnery
Publishing, 1997), p. 221.

[249] "he kept a file inside on the Waco invasion . . . Foster used a safe . . . two
folders from the NSA . . ."
Senate Whitewater Special Committee: Deposition of Deborah
Gorham, June 23, 1995. Cited in Ambrose Evans-Pritchard, *The
Secret Life of Bill Clinton* (Regnery Publishing, 1997), p. 221.

[250] "two large envelopes . . . Janet Reno . . . William Kennedy . . ."
Ibid. Cited in Ambrose Evans-Pritchard, *The Secret Life of Bill
Clinton* (Regnery Publishing, 1997), p. 196.

[251] "Dennis Sculimbrene . . . 'When you are troubled by something . . .'"
Carl Limbacher, "New Documentary Links First Lady and Foster
to Waco," *Newsmax.com*, Nov. 4, 1999.

[252] "T. March Bell . . . 'pressure that came from the first lady of the United
States.'"
Ibid.

[253] "phone logs suggest . . . It was she, Bell's source claims . . ."
Ibid.

[254] "Danny Coulson . . . 'started by gas grenades . . .'"
Jeff Stein, "Delta Team at Waco? A former CIA official says
Army Commandos played a role in the deadly standoff," *Salon*,
August 28, 1999.

[255] "Gene Cullen . . . 'I was surprised at the amount of involvement . . .'"

Ibid.

[256] Editorial, *Wall Street Journal*, Aug. 6, 1993.

[257] "largest city with illegal gambling operations in the country . . ."
Sam Smith, "Arkansas Connections: A time line of the rise and fall of Clinton and friends," (Year 1960 of Timeline), *Progressive Review*, 1998.

[258] "The group discussed "large quantities of drugs . . ."
Sam Smith, "Arkansas Connections: A time line of the rise and fall of Clinton and friends," (Year 1990 of Timeline), *Progressive Review*, 1998. See also Ambrose Evans-Pritchard, *The Secret Life of Bill Clinton* (Regnery Publishing, 1997), p. 349.

[259] "Barry Seal was flying weapons . . . in return he is allowed to smuggle . . ."
Handwritten diary of Arkansas State Trooper Russell Welch. Cited in Ambrose Evans-Pritchard, *The Secret Life of Bill Clinton* (Regnery Publishing, 1997), p. 328.

[260] "embraced by then Vice-President and former CIA chief George H.W. Bush . . ."
Sam Smith, "Arkansas Connections: A time line of the rise and fall of Clinton and friends," (Year 1984 of Timeline), *Progressive Review*, 1998.

[261] "Pilot Terry Reed worked with Seal . . ."
Reed gives his entire story in a lengthy video interview: *The Mena Connection: A Documentary by Terry Reed*, Jan. 1995, Reed Court Offensive; PO Box K; White Springs, FL; 32096. See also Ambrose Evans-Pritchard, *The Secret Life of Bill Clinton* (Regnery Publishing, 1997), p. 349.

[262] "Reed was dangerous due to his testimony of a private meeting . . ."
Ibid.

[263] "the dozen roses he brought her . . ."
Videotaped interview of Janis Reed. *The Mena Connection: A Documentary by Terry Reed*, Jan. 1995, Reed Court Offensive; PO Box K; White Springs, FL; 32096. See also Ambrose Evans-Pritchard, *The Secret Life of Bill Clinton* (Regnery Publishing, 1997), p. 345.

[264] "my investment banker."
Evans-Pritchard, p. 346-347.

[265] "hundreds of millions in bonds . . ."
Ambrose Evans-Pritchard, *The Secret Life of Bill Clinton* (Regnery Publishing, 1997), p. 310-311.

[266] "meeting their mother, Virginia Kelly, at the Hot Springs horse racing track . . ."
Ambrose Evans-Pritchard, *The Secret Life of Bill Clinton* (Regnery Publishing, 1997), p. 291.

[267] "convicted of social distribution of cocaine . . ."
Ambrose Evans-Pritchard, *The Secret Life of Bill Clinton* (Regnery Publishing, 1997), p. 290.

[268] "He was doing a line . . ."
Ibid.

[269] "She was sentenced to 31 years . . ."
Ambrose Evans-Pritchard, *The Secret Life of Bill Clinton* (Regnery Publishing, 1997), p. 260.

[270] "He slid down the wall into a garbage can . . ."
Ambrose Evans-Pritchard, *The Secret Life of Bill Clinton* (Regnery Publishing, 1997), p. 262.

[271] "Coroner Famy Malak ruled the boys were killed by the train . . ."
Ambrose Evans-Pritchard, *The Secret Life of Bill Clinton* (Regnery Publishing, 1997), p. 265.

[272] "the head of James Milam . . . decapitated with a knife . . ."
Ambrose Evans-Pritchard, *The Secret Life of Bill Clinton* (Regnery Publishing, 1997), p. 266.

[273] "ruled "blunt trauma" by Malak . . ."
Ibid.

[274] "and later returned with blood all over him . . ."
Ambrose Evans-Pritchard, *The Secret Life of Bill Clinton* (Regnery Publishing, 1997), p. 264.

[275] "harassed the DEA officer . . ."
Ambrose Evans-Pritchard, *The Secret Life of Bill Clinton* (Regnery Publishing, 1997), p. 258.

[276] "convicted by a jury for racketeering, extortion and drug dealing."
Ambrose Evans-Pritchard, *The Secret Life of Bill Clinton* (Regnery Publishing, 1997), p. 255.

[277] "Patsy Thomasson, a major Clinton backer, worked as Lasater's top assistant . . ."
Ambrose Evans-Pritchard, *The Secret Life of Bill Clinton* (Regnery Publishing, 1997), p. 292.

[278] "had Roger drive Dan's limo . . ."
Sam Smith, "Arkansas Connections: A time line of the rise and fall of Clinton and friends," (Year 1996 of Timeline), *Progressive Review*, 1998.

[279] "worked as a stable hand at a Lasater's horse farm . . ."
Ambrose Evans-Pritchard, *The Secret Life of Bill Clinton* (Regnery Publishing, 1997), p. 292.

[280] "He's got a nose like a vacuum cleaner."
Ambrose Evans-Pritchard, *The Secret Life of Bill Clinton* (Regnery Publishing, 1997), p. 241.

[281] "Roger's sentence was reduced to one year . . ."
Joyce Milton, *The First Partner: Hillary Rodham Clinton*, (Perennial, 1999), p. 167.

[282] "Lasater was awarded a $30 million bond issue . . ."
Sam Smith, "Arkansas Connections: A time line of the rise and fall of Clinton and friends," (Year 1985 of Timeline), *Progressive Review*, 1998.

[283] "the Feds hired the Rose Law firm . . . 'glaring conflict of interest' . . ."
Ambrose Evans-Pritchard, *The Secret Life of Bill Clinton* (Regnery Publishing, 1997), p. 311.

[284] "Governor Clinton pardoned him."
Ambrose Evans-Pritchard, *The Secret Life of Bill Clinton* (Regnery Publishing, 1997), p. 297.

[285] "That's Lasater's deal."
Ambrose Evans-Pritchard, *The Secret Life of Bill Clinton* (Regnery Publishing, 1997), p. 341-342.

[286] "Genovese crime family . . . 'Svengali' . . . consigliorie . . ."
Edward Klein, *The Truth about Hillary*, (Sentinal, 2005), p. 27-28.

[287] "probe by organized crime investigators . . . Meyer Lansky . . .Carlo Gambino . . ."
Clarke, Knowlton and Turley, *Failure of the Public Trust*, (McCabe Publishing, 1999), p. 39-40.

[288] "his own elbow had been broken the day before . . ."
   Wall Street Journal, editorial page, July 19, 1993.

[289] "assassinated by a top-secret team of navy hit men."
   Joyce Milton, *The First Partner: Hillary Rodham Clinton*,
(Perennial, 1999), p. 303.

[290] "a memo eventually surfaced showing Hillary was behind the firing . . ."
   Joyce Milton, *The First Partner: Hillary Rodham Clinton*,
(Perennial, 1999), p. 289.

[291] "Foster was still dragging his feet . . . blind trust . . . whitewater property .
. ."
   Ambrose Evans-Pritchard, *The Secret Life of Bill Clinton* (Regnery
Publishing, 1997), p. 222.

[292] "a file on Bill's infidelities . . ."
   Ambrose Evans-Pritchard, *The Secret Life of Bill Clinton* (Regnery
Publishing, 1997), p. 243.

[293] "head of security for the Clinton-Gore campaign . . ."
   Ambrose Evans-Pritchard, *The Secret Life of Bill Clinton* (Regnery
Publishing, 1997), p. 234.

[294] "It happened to be Roger Clinton . . ."
   Ambrose Evans-Pritchard, *The Secret Life of Bill Clinton* (Regnery
Publishing, 1997), p. 239.

[295] "'This is really good shit!' Bill told his brother."
   Evans-Pritchard, p. 239.

[296] "raucous orgasms"
   Ambrose Evans-Pritchard, *The Secret Life of Bill Clinton* (Regnery
Publishing, 1997), p. 243.

[297] "Jerry Parks had been hired separately by Vince Foster . . ."
   Ambrose Evans-Pritchard, *The Secret Life of Bill Clinton* (Regnery
Publishing, 1997), p. 246.

[298] "such as monitoring and filming the condo of Gennifer Flowers . . ."
   Ambrose Evans-Pritchard, *The Secret Life of Bill Clinton* (Regnery
Publishing, 1997), p. 236.

[299] "I'm a dead man"
   Ambrose Evans-Pritchard, *The Secret Life of Bill Clinton* (Regnery
Publishing, 1997), p. 233.

300 "Foster called the house on a regular basis . . ."
> Ambrose Evans-Pritchard, *The Secret Life of Bill Clinton* (Regnery Publishing, 1997), p. 245.

301 "Jerry was also a friend of Barry Seal . . ."
> Ibid.

302 "filled with $100 bills . . . said I should 'forget what I'd seen.'"
> Ambrose Evans-Pritchard, *The Secret Life of Bill Clinton* (Regnery Publishing, 1997), p. 246-247.

303 "the files contained 'plenty to hurt both of them . . ."
> Ambrose Evans-Pritchard, *The Secret Life of Bill Clinton* (Regnery Publishing, 1997), p. 247.

304 "You can't give Hillary those files . . . she's capable of doing anything . . ."
> Ambrose Evans-Pritchard, *The Secret Life of Bill Clinton* (Regnery Publishing, 1997), p. 248.

305 "We can trust Hil. Don't worry"
> Ibid.

306 "None of the behavior following Vince Foster's suicide . . . I felt endangered . . ."
> Grand Jury Testimony of Linda Tripp, July 28, 1998, quoted in "Tripp Testifies of Foster Death Cover-up; Murder of Jerry Parks," *Newsmax.com*, Oct. 8, 1999.

307 "there was a 'flurry of activity . . . it was something they chose not to speak about . . ."
> Ibid.

308 "someone burglarized their home . . . Gary peeked at it once . . ."
> Ambrose Evans-Pritchard, *The Secret Life of Bill Clinton* (Regnery Publishing, 1997), p. 236.

309 Correspondence between Attorney General William French Smith and CIA Director WIlliam Casey, Feb. 11, 1982 and March 2, 1982. Cited in Congressional Record, May 7, 1998, Page H2970. Cited in Catherine Austin Fitts, "Dillon, Read & Co. Inc. and the Aristocracy of Prison Profits, Part II: Narco Dollars in Mena and L.A, Insider Deals at Dillon Read and Massive Mortgage Fraud in HUD related to Iran Contra.", Narco News Bulletin, Issue 40, Article 1650, March 1, 2006 <narconews.com>

310 Ibid, see footnote 8.

Postscript

[311] "in the room with him when he died . . ."
Author's interview with Hugh Turley.

[312] "Mark Tuohey joined a law firm in Houston . . ."
Ambrose Evans-Pritchard, *The Secret Life of Bill Clinton* (Regnery Publishing, 1997), p. 139.

[313] washingtonian.com/2006/01/01/washingtonians-of-the-year-2005-1/

[314] "He later advised Congress to abolish the Office of Independent Counsel . . ."
Clarke, Knowlton and Turley, *Failure of the Public Trust*, (McCabe Publishing, 1999), p. 453-454.

[315] "He is now "Michelle Rodriguez . . ."
Greg Szymanski, "The Cover-Up of Vince Foster's Murder gets Stranger and Stranger," *Artic Beacon*, April 12, 2006.

[316] "It is often the fringe media . . ."
"Death of Vince Foster: Parts 4," Accuracy in Media tape transcription of ABC's *Nightline*: Interview of Reed Irvine by Ted Koppel.

[317] The complete Report is online at the Haithi Trust Digital Library. See https://catalog.hathitrust.org/Record/003263302